Iron Moon

Iron Moon

An Anthology of Chinese Migrant Worker Poetry

Edited by Qin Xiaoyu

Translated by Eleanor Goodman

WHITE PINE PRESS / BUFFALO, NEW YORK

White Pine Press
P.O. Box 236 Buffalo, NY 14201
www.whitepine.org

Publication of this book was made possible, in part, by public funds from the China Classics International Fund; Wu Xiaobo; the New York State Council on the Arts, a State Agency; with funds from the National Endowment for the Arts, which believes that a great nation deserves great art; and with the support of the Amazon Literary Partnership.

Acknowledgments: Poems in this collection have appeared in *Mantis* ("Elegy," Li Hao), *China Labour Bulletin* ("I Swallowed an Iron Moon," "Terracotta Army on the Assembly Line," and "Obituary for a Peanut," Xu Lizhi), *Kyoto Review* ("I Swallowed an Iron Moon," Xu Lizhi), and reprinted in *Technicians of the Sacred* (Expanded Edition), University of California Press ("I Swallowed an Iron Moon" and "Obituary for a Peanut," Xu Lizhi).

The cover image was provided by MeDoc.

Library of Congress Control Number: 2016949218

ISBN: 978-1-945680-03-8

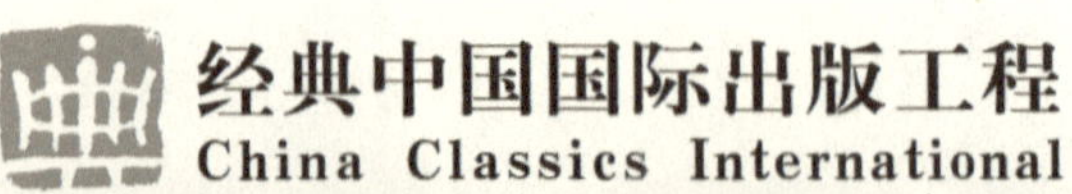

This book was made possible by the generous support of Wu Xiaobo.

Contents

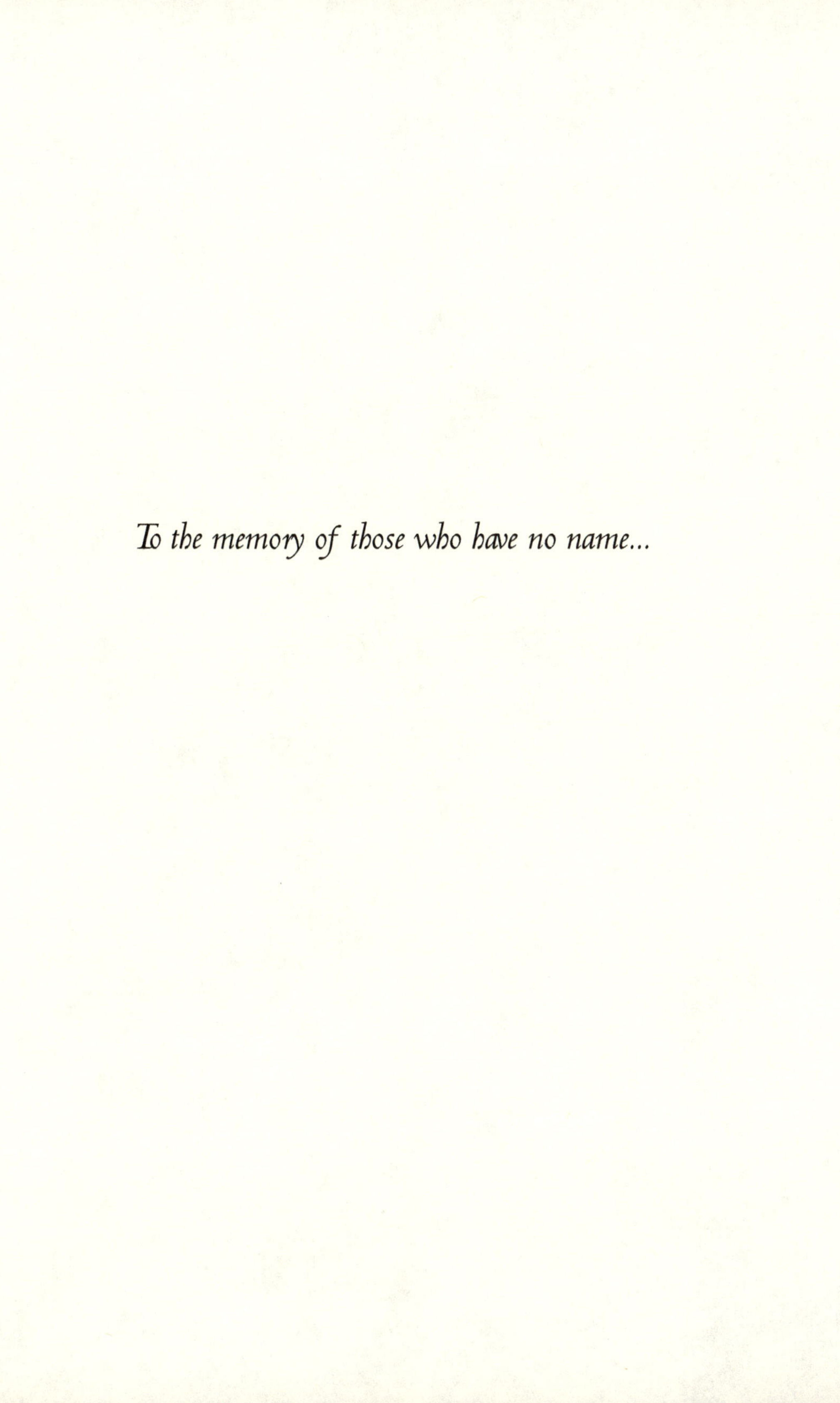

To the memory of those who have no name...

Remembering the Anonymous

Qin Xiaoyu

This anthology originated from a documentary film of the same name. The film, *Iron Moon,* evoked a strong reaction in China, as it follows the lives of several worker-poets working at the lowest levels of the society and suffering the most from globalization. The situations these workers find themselves in, and the poetry they write, represent problems that are not unique to China, but rather have implications for countries across the world.

The term "iron moon" comes from a poem by Xu Lizhi, who was born in 1990 and worked in a Foxconn factory making Apple products until his suicide in 2014. An assembly line worker, he wrote more than two hundred largely unhappy poems before his death. Perhaps his best known poem is "I Swallowed an Iron Moon":

> I swallowed an iron moon
> they called it a screw
>
> I swallowed industrial wastewater and unemployment forms
> bent over machines, our youth died young
>
> I swallowed labor, I swallowed poverty
> swallowed pedestrian bridges, swallowed this rusted-out life
>
> I can't swallow any more
> everything I've swallowed roils up in my throat
>
> I spread across my country
> a poem of shame

The iron moon is a powerful symbol of the hardships so-called "migrant workers" such as Xu Lizhi face in their daily lives. The concept of the migrant worker first appeared in China in 1984, when the researcher Zhang Yulin began surveying the development of towns and cities, which, along with the rise of industry, brought large numbers of rural residents from the countryside into the cities for the first time. This group of people became known as migrant workers, pointing to their status as outsiders in their own country. The policy that underpinned this movement of popuation was "Document I," presented by the national government on January 1, 1984, which allowed rural residents to take their grain rations and go out to look for work.

Despite the fact that such workers have existed for quite some time, "migrant worker" is a new term. In the mid-nineteenth century, with the advent of industrialization, many Western farmers left their land to enter factories and mines as a source of cheap labor, and the same is essentially true for the first migrant workers in China. Generally speaking, up until the 1950s, rural residents in China had the basic freedom to move to find work, but this changed suddenly in 1956, when the central government and related departments issued nine documents in quick succession that were intended to restrict the movement of rural residents. These restrictions were made official law on January 9, 1958 in the form of Resolution 91. Item 10 of the "Republic of China Household Registration Act" read: "Any rural resident seeking to move to the city must possess employment documents from that city's labor department, proof of official acceptance by a university or school, or proof of permission from the city's household registration department." This legislation effectively made it illegal for over 85% of the rural population to change residence at will, but few people questioned whether it contravened the article of the 1954 constitution guaranteeing "the right of self-determination of residence and internal movement." Why did the government wish to put up such strict barriers between rural and urban areas in the first place?

Scholars hold differing opinions. Some say it was simply a necessary stage in the process of industrialization under a socialist system, corresponding to the country's reality of having "a large population in poverty." Some say it was a countermeasure to the large number of rural residents who, in response to natural disasters, differences in the standard of living, and so on, chose to pour into the cities, creating an "urban problem." Still other scholars say it was intended to stop the loss of the rural labor force, in order to ensure agricultural production. I find the scholar Zhang Yulin's response most convincing. He rejects the aforementioned explanations for several reasons. First, India, which was facing a similar situation, did not implement a system of registered permanent residence, while socialist countries such as Russia, which did not have an "urban problem," did employ systems to control the free movement of their rural populations. Second, he rejects the idea that the government wanted to protect agricultural production levels, because at that time there was excess labor capacity in the countryside. Zhang believes instead that the system of control over permanent residence came from a need to uphold the existing collectivist agricultural system: "It was intended to make the rural population settle down into their rural cooperatives to devote themselves to farm labor to aid in the greater industrialization of the country. The goal was to prevent rural residents from fleeing their cooperatives. In order to consolidate and strengthen those cooperatives, it was necessary to implement such a system. This system had to function like a security wall around a concentration camp: whether a willing or reluctant participant, no matter how unhappy and desperate to leave a person became, there was no possibility of escape." The fact that in the 1980s, rural residents were relatively free to leave the countryside and indeed did, reinforces this. Zhang Yulin goes a step further to point out that in the early 1980s, people's communes gradually weakened and began to collapse, and accordingly the rural areas did not have to depend so heavily on restrictions on the movements of the population. Only then did the large-scale movement of this population become a possibility.

This situation can also be understood from the angle of the systematic integration of industry and agricultural production. In the 1950s, due to the requirements industrialization presented under a planned economy, rural residents were confined to the land by the permanent residence registration system and collectivized farming. Thirty years later, as the country moved toward industrializing in a market economy and there was a need for mass cheap labor, rural residents were allowed to move out of the countryside, becoming a source of migrant labor. The country and private enterprises once again relied upon the permanent residence registration system to avoid giving these workers benefits and proper wages, ensuring that labor costs were kept low.

In May of 1990, a Hong Kong-financed factory making raincoats for export to America and Europe caught fire, causing the death of eighteen people. This was the first major fire at a foreign-backed enterprise and it brought the issue of worker safety into the public eye. According to government statistics, the average number of workers killed in work-related accidents in any given year is around 100,000. With the lack of professional training, inadequate or hazardous worksites, an absence of basic protections, long hours and extremely demanding work, China leads the world in workplace injuries, occupational diseases, and psychological problems. Nevertheless, it took continuous calls to implement the "Safety Production Law" and "Prevention and Treatment of Occupational Diseases Law," both of which faced considerable resistance. In 1992, Deng Xiaoping went on his southern speaking tour, and in 1993, the central government put out a statement saying that it would vigorously develop the labor market and encouraging excess labor forces from the countryside to move into the cities. This gave rise to a wave of migrant workers that for a time increased exponentially; today, more than 274 million people have contributed in this way to China's economic development. Along with this, however, came a host of problems, including left behind and homeless children, empty-nesters, an increased divorce rate, and so on. These painful stories of abandoned hometowns have become a principle theme for worker-poets.

Similarly, in 1992, the State Council put out a document, "View on the Reform of Custody and Return," which expanded a program that involved police taking people into custody and forcing them to return to their legal residence. The program went from targeting vagrant beggars to targeting "people lacking one of three things": a legal ID, a fixed residence, or a steady income. As the program expanded, holding facilities began to concoct new fees, and situations of forced labor and illegal detention arose with them. The worker-poets Bing Ma and Chi Moshu both have experience with being in custody, and Bing Ma even wrote an exposé poem called "May 9-10: Mengzi Road in Shanghai, at the Station under the Custody and Return Program." In 2003, after an incident in which the worker Sun Zhigang died in custody, the brutal Custody and Return system finally came to an end.

After the global financial crisis in 2008, there was an outflux of labor back to the countryside, and the development model of using cheap labor with virtually no protections faced a severe challenge. The State Council's 2014 View on Further Promoting the Reform of the Household Registration System was a clear signal that the binary registration system dividing city and countryside would be abolished; in 2015, household registration was unified across regions, temporary residence permits were abolished, and a separate residence permit system was put into effect. Perhaps when these reforms actually take effect, the term "migrant worker" will finally disappear.

The term "migrant worker" itself has long been subject of debate. With the slow awakening of political consciousness, some workers have begun to oppose its usage. Their main argument is that the term is discriminatory, since it is often used in a derogatory context and carries a pejorative connotation. However, the origin of the term is in fact found in sympathetic scholarly work that describes this relatively new phenomenon. Not only was it devoid of pejorative connotation, it was intended to be a term of admiration. It also expresses the circumstances of these traveling laborers, which is one reason the term gained popularity. It is a highly inclusive concept, while still indicating that this group's fundamental difficulties stem from the sharp division between city and countryside. These migrant workers must cross the literal and invisible barriers between these two worlds, and continually pay the price for it.

The poetry of migrant workers is frequently called "labor poetry." "Labor" implies working for a boss and being paid piecemeal. In the language of a capitalist marketplace economy, which entered the country via Hong Kong to Guangdong in the 1980s, the term implies the commercialization of the labor force. Along with the marketization of China's economy, and the expansion of capitalism, such terms gradually replaced the older socialist labor system vocabulary, and began to underpin how workers view their own work. The romanticization of migrant worker poetry has come from a kind of exploitation of and encroachment on the image of the laborer; however, the use of "labor poetry" is also problematic, as it emphasizes a specific social role and combines workers of different types with different lives into one category. It also presents a fantasy that is easily exploited, and too readily turned into a story of social harmony and achieving one's dreams.

Migrant worker poetry has its origins in the wave of migratory labor that began in the 1990s, when a very small number of workers with an interest in literature or culture began to write about the experiences they had in factories far from their hometowns. This created a separate category of poetry, written by those in the lowest rungs of society. Among them, Xie Xiangnan stands out. In 1992, not long after Deng Xiaoping's southern speaking tour, Xie left school and his hometown in Hunan to travel to Zhejiang to find work. That same year, he began to write poetry. Over the next few years, he bounced between the Pearl River Delta and his hometown, working as a construction worker, assembler at a toy factory, docker at an electroplate factory, fitter at a paper plant, machine-tool operator at an electronics factory, and so on. This life of constantly changing jobs and moving back and forth between countryside and city is a common experience among migrant workers. These worker poets resemble traditional Chinese "itinerant intellectuals," leaving their homes to seek a livelihood in the cities, concealed at the bottom of society, undergoing the hardships of their trade. Unlike others in the same situation, these poets have a conscious desire to write; and unlike traditional literati or contemporary intellectuals, they frequently must make their living doing something they despise. In their writing, they tend not to be concerned with grand, abstract issues and their language is typically not highly refined; but they come from a particular and important angle, which combined with their rich personal experiences, can paint a powerful picture of lives that few readers know.

The poet Xie Xiangnan once slept for a week on a stone bench outside the Guangzhou train station, and wrote several poems testifying to the waves of migrant laborers. "Guangzhou Train Station, March, 1996" mentions two paintings that appear in Chinese middle school history textbooks, namely "Liberty Leading the People" and "Lenin on the Rostrum." These paintings lead to the same question: Was it the people's free will that led to the first waves of migrant workers, or was it a result of the speeches Deng Xiaoping gave as he traveled in the south? Could it be both at once? Western culture allows for female symbolic leaders, while in Eastern socialist systems, leaders tend to be represented as male sages or kings. In Delacroix's painting, Lady Liberty and the revolutionaries run together through the smoke of the battlefield; in contrast, in the second painting, a towering godlike Lenin faces a square filled with an indistinct featureless crowd, delivering his message from on high. Xie Xiangnan sees the situation at the Guangzhou Train Station as similar: "There was a huge crowd at the Guangzhou train station in March 1996 too / the bags piled on the square were like packages of explosives / and I almost imagined the digital clock towering overhead / was our beloved Lenin." The language of the revolution has already changed and the world itself has undergone a metamorphosis: what the "digital clock" points to is a new historical moment. Xie's poem "Listening to a Song During an Endless Train Ride" does not involve as many historical or contemporary allusions and metaphors. Instead it describes in straightforward language the blind enthusiasm that brings migrants to the cities, embodying their resolute attitude with his short, powerful lines. But having paid such a high price to leave their hometowns, what will they do in the cities? The absurd but completely realistic answer is: "We'll see when we get there."

What greets them there is not a "beautiful new world," but rather the underbelly of the city. Unlike purely literary writers or scholars merely interested in the poor, the poverty that these worker-poets describe constitutes their daily experiences. The entrance to this world is the chaos of a train station, and, as Bing Ma describes, the train station used for the Custody and Return program is the seamy exit. The migrant workers and poor residents are the main inhabitants of this world, and shantytowns are its central regions. Many companies offer dormitories to their workers, but this is less of a benefit than a way to control workers even during their time off. As such, it is primarily intended to raise production rates, as the workers are little more than prisoners in the strict dormitory environment. Given the chance, many workers would rather rent an apartment with a spouse or friends, especially the younger workers, who tend to desire more personal space. But the only choice aside from company dormitories seems to be shantytowns that have sprung up nearby, of which Xie Xiangnnan writes: "you worked all day and then did overtime / in the stairwells of shantytowns, you passionately / kissed your lovers" (Girls Buried in Shenzhen). Or this from Tian Xiaoyin's "Makeng Shantytown": "Hallucinogenic ads on bathroom walls, profusions of headlines made by massage parlor lamps / scalping and the scalpers are taken in by the era, by the X Bureau. . . ." Another example is Tang Yihong's "Tear-filled Paradise":

> During the day no one cries in pain, and no one dares cry out
> with their bit of pleasure at night. No one dares cry out.
> So many bodies and souls hide themselves like thieves in the night
> and they're often dragged out from the nighttime's smidgen
> of pleasure. Bare-chested, they huddle
> in rows under the eaves to accept interrogation. Interrogate
> their identity as couples of temporary workers, working couples,
> couples who've been worked.
>
> Wastewater ditches. Garbage dumps. Darkness and damp.
> Advertisements for itinerant doctors.
> Impotent and desolate, cold words, blotted-out sky, it all makes
> people feel
> that's who they are. Some of them must be that way.

These shantytowns are like festering wounds on the city's body, hidden by the shimmering image of progress. In the eyes of city officials, the people living in these places are disorderly, crammed into buildings without permits, piling up garbage. The infrastructure is substandard, and there are problems with public order. They are simply blights on the city, a chronic illness that impedes its progress. But how many of the people who have labored with their own bodies to create the city have no choice but to live in these places? They are a kind of purgatory, a "tear-filled paradise." As much as the workers may curse the shantytowns, they still hope the city will not uproot them.

The poet Zheng Xiaoqiong uses the shantytowns as a kind of metaphor for the spirit of the workers. Just as these places are neither completely rural nor completely urban, these workers are neither salaried workers nor farmers. They work in the city but are not accepted by it. Poets Chen Nianxi, Zheng Xiaoqiong, Cheng Peng, Ceng Xuqiang, and Xu Lizhi all express the conviction that they are writing for the poor, from the standpoint of the poor. Another important element to this situation is globalization. This is a critical moment in history, in which workers find themselves laboring in "global factories" and worker-poets are able to post their poems on the internet. Not only do they work at one end of the global production line, keeping the screws turning, but their lives are thrown into the middle of it and are profoundly affected by the power and cruelty of global capitalism.

Yet these worker-poets rarely write from a sense of righteousness and self-sacrifice. Rather, they tend to believe themselves to be mere temporary workers, hicks, nobodies, and the frequent metaphor of the screw expresses this feeling of powerlessness. Their poverty and the nature of their work reinforces a lack of self-worth. Today, industry has already developed to the point that workers no longer need to master any particular skill. Complex production systems are run by high-tech automation, while across-the-board systematization has meant that workers are locked into one step of the process, doing the same simple motion over and over, day in and day out. The intelligence and skill of these workers have been made obsolete, and they find themselves just screws holding together the enormous production machine. These 'screws' experience tremendous pressure (just as a literal screw undergoes tightening) and pain. One could even say that workers poetry is essentially a kind of literature of trauma. Aside from the trials and humiliations of living at the bottom of society, this poetry has two main themes: the alienated work of factories and the hidden and lasting anguish of leaving one's hometown.

Judging by the the poetry of these worker-poets, the factories lead to an exhausting and painful process of alienation and lives devoid of beauty, just links in the chain of globalized production. Zheng Xiaoqiong and Xu Lizhi both employ premature aging to express the damage capitalist production inflicts on people. In "Woman Worker: Youth Pinned to a Station," Zheng writes: "flowing products and interlocking time swallowed up quickly / aging ten years flowing past like water." The speed of the assembly line is the speed of their aging.

Xu Lizhi wrote his first 'worker poem' four months after beginning to work at Foxconn—the largest Apple factory in the word. "Sculpture on the Assembly Line" describes how the rules of the factory and the cruelty of the mechanized system remolded his body, pinning him to his post and seeming to age him within the space of a few months. Two years later and accustomed to factory life, Xu wrote "Terracotta Army on the Assembly Line." This poem has no emotive language or sense of self-pity, only a scathing, straightforward description. The "sculpture" has become a "terracotta army," and the accusatory force is even greater. Although they both point to a deep alienation, "sculpture" focuses on the self, while "terracotta army" indicates an enormous anonymous group. Unlike a typical sculpture, the terracotta soldiers represent dead bodies and are funereal sacrifices, uniform and alarming in number, standing in eternal combat readiness. This is just like the workers, functioning under the nearly militarized pressures of a despotic industrial empire, who are "all at the ready / silently awaiting their orders / and when the bell rings / they're sent back to the Qin." Are these workers then a "terracotta army" who have been forced into military service, or are they simply beasts of burden? Are they members of the modern industrialized society, or slaves in a traditional imperial social system? Marx of course described this process of alienation and enslavement by the system of production; far from simply repeating the argument, Xu Lizhi absorbs the critique into his poetic form. The "line" in the beginning of the poem—"Along the line stands"—of course refers to the assembly line, but the poem itself is a kind of thin line that mimics a product traveling down the assembly line, as the names are listed one per line. When the bell sounds, the worker-soldiers begin to move, and in an instant, these participants in modern globalization are returned to the ancient Qin dynasty, becoming slaves or sacrificial objects.

Screws, worker ID cards, work numbers, stations, assembly lines, uniforms, order forms, iron and steel, workshops, machine consoles, sulfuric acid, presses, antistatic clothing, antistatic gloves, denatured alcohol, solvents, dust, die molds, controls, gears, blueprints, coolants, anti-rust oils, fire doors, electrical components, tool bits. The abstract Marxist concept of "relations of production" is transformed by these concrete details of the factory into "production relationships." The worker-poets use these details to express the alienated work that goes on in these factories and inside the production system, exposing the domination of capitalism from the inside. They also write about injury, occupational diseases and even the unnecessary deaths of young workers. In this anthology alone, Tang Yihong, Chi Moshu, Zhang Shougang, Lizi, Zheng Xiaoqing, and Shu Zhishui all write about severed fingers. Xie Xiangnan's "Work Accident Joint Investigative Report" is written in the style of an actual accident report, and describes an incident involving a woman worker who has "been working continuously for twelve hours." When injured, she does not scream or cry, but merely leaves clutching her own severed finger. The indifference of capitalism can be seen in the fact that there is no use even in crying out. Worker-poets do not only write about such injuries; they themselves suffer injuries and occupational diseases. Liu Dongyang lost the tip of a finger to a plate shearing machine, and Zhang Shougang had four of his fingers cut off when he lost control of a lathe. The painful descriptions found here in *Iron Moon* rival anything seen across the two thousand years of Chinese poetry.

The worst that these workers face is potential death from accidents or occupational diseases. Chen Nianxi labored as a demolitions worker in mines for sixteen years and narrowly escaped death many times. Inside deep mountain mines, he would drill a hole, fill it with explosive powder, and then set it off, blowing up the rock. He tells of once working with some employees of a state-owned enterprise and realizing that they made more than he did for much less effort, revealing the class disparity built into the relationships between workers themselves. In Chen's "Yang Sai and Yang Zai," he plays with the similarity in names between a gold ore mine (Yang Sai) and one of his coworkers (Yang Zai), who "ran too fast and got ahead of the explosives / and ran into a cloud of smoke." The smoke is that of the explosives, and also of the mystery of death. Chen refers back to the famous lines of Du Fu, "the spoiled wine and meat of the rich, bones freezing the road," in his lines "I've heard they built a tavern in the eastern valley / while the flags of the dead crowd the western slopes." The times change, but the situation of the poor does not, and the disparity of wealth continues. The last line of the poem reads: "the snow is gone   but winter is still here."

For the worker-poets, the theme of death expresses a kind of floating despair, crushing defeats, alienation, and deep traumas. As Xu Lizhi writes in "Laborer Entering the City":

Many years ago
with a bag on his back
he walked into
this bustling city

high-spirited and daring

Many years later
he carried his own ashes in his hands
standing at the city's
crossroads

looking around hopelessly

In a few lines, the "laborer" is turned into an abstract symbol stripped of individualism, and indeed because of this, the figue can serve as a symbol of all workers. The poem mirrors itself: the first half outlines a typical hopeful young worker; the second half skillfully paints the picture of the painfully absurd outcome. The absurdity cannot hide the grief and despair of the laborer's fate. Taken together, the two halves of the poem form the silhouette of any one of the workers coming into the city, or serve as a nameless memorial to them all. The ending presents a conundrum: at this particular "crossroads" of history, which direction should the city and these workers take?

Xu's "Obituary for a Peanut" simply copies text directly from the label of a peanut butter jar. Read as an obituary, however, it creates a highly disturbing effect: if the production of the peanut butter means the death of the peanut, the producers are murderers, the factory is the crime scene, and the production date at the end of the poem is the time of death. The crushing of the peanut perfectly symbolizes the crushing fate these workers experience. Simply by adding a title, the poet creates a postmodern poem out of a peanut butter label, without any artifice and replete with repudiation and emotive power. This poem, like "Laborer Entering the City," employs a striking poetic form, yet they are not examples of mere formalism, but rather operate from great expressive necessity. Worker-poets such as Xu Lizhi are not highly literary writers who belong to a particular poetic faction; their poetry instead springs from the necessities of reality.

Around 2 p.m. on September 30, 2014, Xu Lizhi jumped from the seventeenth floor of a building in Longhua, Shenzhen, "to spread across my country / a poem of shame." At midnight on October 1 (the National Day holiday in China) a post titled "A New Day," which he had set to go up automatically, appeared on his weibo blog. Opinions vary about why he chose to end his life, but I tend to think of it as an expression of the despair young workers at the bottom of society face. In his representative work *Suicide,* Émile Durkheim, one of the founders of modern social theory, attributed suicide to psychological and astronomical factors, along with imitative behavior. Using facts and statistics, Durkheim demonstrated that at first glance the suicide victim's actions seem to be an expression of his or her temperament or particular situation; however, it becomes clear that such actions are in fact an externalization of larger social conditions. His colleague Pierre Bourdieu also pointed out the sociological factors in personal pain. The personal misfortune borne by individuals actually embody deep conflicts within the society and are at essence a kind of "social suffering." Xu Lizhi chose the most popular way at Foxconn to kill himself: jumping out of a building. His poem "A Screw Plunges to the Ground" describes this with eerie calm.

Although male migrant workers outnumber female migrant workers by a ratio of approximately two to one, there are more women than men working in factories producing consumer goods for export. This is partly because the labor-intensive assembly lines require neither highly specialized skills nor great physical strength. Female workers also have a reputation for being diligent, able to withstand hardship, and easier to manage, and so they are welcomed by companies. In the abrupt rise of manufacturing in China, it is no exaggeration to say that women workers do hold up half of the sky. These women are subject to all of the difficulties of male workers, but they also face additional problems, including fertility issues, sexual harassment, and more trouble finding work after being let go. Should male worker-poets take it upon themselves to describe the difficulties female workers face? For example, several poems by male poets in this volume mention menstruation, while only Zheng Xiaoqiong, a woman poet, mentions "missed periods" ("A Product's Story") and "a lifetime of irregular periods" ("Woman Worker: Youth Fixed to a Station"). The natural rhythms of a woman's body and the industrial clock are sure to come into conflict: in addition to the long working hours and psychological pressures, the insufficiently varied diets and contact with chemicals cause all manner of menstrual problems. Some companies have even used "medicines" to control women's menstrual cycles, seen by some scholars as the apex of "menstrual politics." Women migrant workers are without a doubt the best chroniclers of these experiences; it is extremely unfortunate, then, that very few women have joined the ranks of worker-poets. In this book, there are only four female poets represented. This lack of parity is only one indication that women are still treated as inferior in the countryside, where the patriarchal system still dictates. Girls are taught to be timid and are forced into silence, even after they have left home. The women poets in this book have already shown great courage in expressing their experiences and attitudes in the face of this oppression.

If women have a natural aesthetic sense and have been taught to be timid, tragedy is sure to occur when these characteristics come into contact with the cruel and unyielding world of the factory. In "Close as Fingers," Lizi describes a female migrant worker who works year in and year out with "the assembly line's copper widgets and iron widgets." These cold objects cannot obliterate her appreciation of beauty, and even her callouses can "flower" open.

> Who knew that ten fingers could flower
> into callouses, that over and over they work
> the assembly line's copper widgets and iron widgets
> but still the lines of her palms
> carry a faint silken scent
>
> The callous blossoms drop into dreams
> and start to savor a relationship as close as fingers
> she starts calling and calling for her loved ones
> faraway lamps light up and then darken again
> the road is like an assembly line, stretching out into the distance

It is clear that the objects of the assembly line and the poet's aesthetic sense are incompatible, but she is not worn down by this. Instead, Lizi's aesthetic appreciation for the world helps her transcend her environment and eases the dullness and difficulty of the work. In the midst of a hard factory life, she maintains a "faint silken scent," which can be read as a metaphor for romantic desire. But this is also the basis for the tragedy of the poem, as her daydreaming leads to the accident that results in a severed finger. What saves her turns out to be what destroys her.

The response of many women workers to the hard life they face is to become hard themselves, either consciously or unconsciously. In "Rocks by the Road" Shu Zhishui describes the workers as essentially tumbleweed, ending up floating "down onto machines in a strange place, down onto assembly lines," where they are "beaten, screwed tight, nailed up." Perhaps because Zheng Xiaoqiong ended up in a hardware factory working as a hole-puncher, she picks up a more industrial image, that of iron. As with Xu Lizhi's 'Iron Moon,' iron has many implications in her poems. It symbolizes the workers' silent labor and their lack of voice: "they move slowly / turning, bending down, silent as cast iron," ("Life"), "cast iron—the silent language of workers," ("Language"). It represents the cruelty of reality and the difficulty of living amid it: "at night who / claims life's past and future in the middle of their ironlike lives," ("Iron"). It also implies lingering traumas: "the crimping and memories of iron sheets," ("Language"). Iron will rust, but in the factory, rust is something that must be gotten rid of, just like a person's natural timidity: "iron reveals rusty cowardice and timidity," ("Iron"). All of these symbolic uses point to the way in which workers, and in particular women, are forced to conform to their environment as the iron is forced into particular shapes.

In the factory, women also face losing their gender distinctions in the dehumanizing atmosphere: "this life of a lost name and gender," ("Life"). Yet iron most fundamentally represents a tenacity of will and a fighting spirit, and Zheng Xiaoqiong seeks to become iron in order to fight an "iron empire." This is also a kind of alienation, but a self-determined one.

In addition to the trials of living in a strange city and working difficult temporary jobs, worker-poets often also address leaving their hometowns, another source of pain. Working as a migrant worker implies abandoning one's parents and spouse, and the lifestyle itself leads workers to miss home all the more. Chen Nianxi articulates this in his poem to his son, composed from "two thousand miles from home on a barren hill":

Son
your clear gaze
sees through words and numbers
sees through the Transformers

but it can't see the reality
I want you to put down your books and look at the world
but I fear you would really see it

Chen's son is one of those who has been left behind by his parents. In China, such children number over sixty million, or more than a fifth of the total child population. Without the care of their parents, many of these children show signs of emotional and behavioral problems. Tang Yihong speaks to this in his poem "It Seems I'm Really His Father," which describes his son hiding behind his grandmother to size him up: "It seems I'm not his father." When the neighbor boy happily runs circles around him, "It seems I'm really his father." The poet describes in plain language his own experience, yet the two "it seems" add a distinct note of tragedy, pointing to the larger troubles the countryside faces. These troubles do not boil down to a single issue; industrialization and the resulting migration of workers has presented an enormous challenge to the traditional rural family that has persisted for thousands of years, helping to destroy the fundamental social structure of the countryside. Cheng Peng's "Abandoned Village" is an elegy for the Chinese countryside, describing how all of the able-bodied workers have left to find work, leaving behind children and the elderly, untended fields, absent teachers, and a deficiency in leadership, both practical and moral. Cheng Peng painstakingly adapts ancient folk songs from the Northern Dynasties (386-581 AD) and lines from the Southern Song lyricist Xin Qiji's "Serene Countryside," using them to create a striking contrast between today's countryside and the rural areas of the past, producing a sense of antithesis. The poem serves as a severe warning, which is entirely warranted. Cheng was born was born in an impoverished family in the countryside near Chongqing. His father died young, and his mother brought up two sons and two daughters on her own. Cheng's brother also died young, his older sister suffered brain damage from misprescribed drugs, and his second sister left to work in the factories: "his oldest daughter leaves to find work and marries someone from a far province, their closeness broken." After graduating from middle school, Cheng Peng went to Guangdong to look for work, but returned empty-handed not long after, to take care of his mother after she was hurt in a car accident. His personal circumstances are no less tragic than those described in the poem.

The pain found in all of these poems is real, although these poems of homesickness also feel illusory, as many of the "hometowns" in the poems have not merely been embellished, but imply a kind of utopia. Reading closely, one realizes that a fulcrum of these poets' pain is a "paradise" like that found in the classic *Book of Songs.* In Tang Yihong's "Returning Home Backward," the poet describes a utopia in which "there's no glory or dishonor, no difference between rich and poor," a veritable rural paradise, and reminiscent also of the working class's ideal communist society. However, far from presenting a positive evolution in history, this "hometown" can only be reached by an impossible "backward" movement, because the place only exists within the mother's body. In this paradise, "there are no tears / and everyone you meet is family," but it remains a place no one can return to. Similarly, Cheng Peng's "Homesickness," while only six lines long, describes the workers' feelings with admirable clarity:

> I live on a screw's sharp word-awn
> I stand on the hard-up painful center of a sentence-edge
> I'm hopelessly squeezed in the pliers' poem-howl
>
> From beginning to middle to end
> the homesick sunset is stuck in rhymes of fatigue and shame
> my thoughts roam toward the future

The poet reminds us here that homesickness does not come from home itself, but rather from the migrant worker's life of "fatigue and shame."

Migrant workers born in the 1960s and 1970s are leading what amounts to an atomized life, and their poetry reflects this "tragic consciousness." Yet, the younger generation of poets with their sense of a common fate and their political consciousness have begun to develop away from this. Zheng Xiaoqing's "Them," Cheng Peng's "Song of Construction Workers," and Shu Zhishui's long piece "Trial" all show this movement, and it reflects trends within the larger migrant worker community a well. Compared to previous generations, the younger workers tend to view the society as unequal and unfair, and they have higher demands for freedom and personal development. Their tolerance for alienated work and autocratic management is lower, their willingness to fight back is greater, and they are more adept at using legal measures and their actions to protect their own interests. The internet has expanded their sense of the world, making it easier to receive and pass on information; at the same time, web-based methods of communication have made it easy for them to keep in touch with each other and mobilize together. While the previous generation saw themselves as farmers, younger workers accept an identity as a worker. According to scholarly research, before 2003, those engaged in labor in the south rarely called themselves "workers," or "working class." They were more apt to call themselves "migrant workers," "peasant workers" or "temps." After 2011, however, many migrant workers clearly defined themselves as "workers" or "employees." Recognizing that they cannot go back home to the countryside, they must begin to fight for their rights as workers. And as soon as they "feel and articulate that they have mutual interests and that those interests are not the same as others, social class is created." In this sense, migrant worker poetry is a literary indicator of this new class that is arising.

In the Spanish border town of Portbou, the Israeli artist Dani Karavan has created a memorial to Walter Benjamin called "Passages," on which is written in five different languages: "It is a more arduous task to honor the memory of anonymous beings than that of famous persons. The construction of history is consecrated to the memory of those who have no name." Benjamin spent his life researching memory, and in his view, the history written by the victors is a typical form of historical violence. Those who suffer oppression, those who are forgotten, are once again crushed in the paeans of history, left out of what is passed down and acknowledged. The poetry of migrant workers in China is an offering "to the memory of those who have no name." To have their individual lives, which have been so often obscured by history written down to be passed on, is a rectification of that history. It can also serve as an inspiration to later generations.

Iron Moon

Li Yongpu (b. 1965, Dengzhou, Henan) left school at fifteen to study furniture-making. In 1985, he was sent to Xinjiang by his work unit and was then transferred to Hubei, Shaanxi, Gansu, and other places. He has worked in brickyards and coal mines, but mainly on construction sites.

Old Zheng

Old Zheng is gone
away from the dropping bricks,
he floated into the enormous empty atmosphere
and sloughed off his shell—
the body in the cemetery
and the uncleaned traces of blood
mingle into a ceremony
of the final dust—ashes

Yesterday, old Zheng wasn't yet gone
at the building site, he stood with me on the scaffolding
staring down at a girl walking beyond the fencing
an angel who put the flowers to shame
he said the world's captivating women
will shorten the lives of the men they meet

Now under the arms of the towering cranes
the walls don't care who old Zheng was
they're being raised layer by layer
and the girl who passed by below   and her electrifying gaze
have nothing to do with him
a sweaty smile at the memory
is secretly absorbed into the shapeless air
in the sky the clouds are clouds and the wind is wind
sometimes I face away from the direction the bricks drop

and try to search upward to the edges of my sight
as the clouds shudder

heavier than dust

Directions

The daily scaffolding
the day and night steel bars and bricks and mortar
no matter how confusing life's direction is
everything moves toward the ever-expanding gray jungle
our schoolbooks teach that three huge mountains were once toppled
and the thriving businesses of today
and the heights of the previous dynasties
chart shockingly similar courses
at worksites the hired foremen and overseers
give directions to make use of every bit of time and space
and force the sky's blue to turn toward limestone's
iron-pale direction while the eight-hour workday
came from the direction of the Paris Commune's bloody struggles
and became the direction of the system's social classes
outside the system the additional four hours given to workers
were fixed to allow for this trifling transplanted
era of capitalism
and its direction of so-called equal justice the night released from its fetters
transforms into a dreamless sleep
and any dreams that do come are of exhaustion and pain
the direction of the blood and sweat and of a postponed work break
while the direction of a mother's spring and of the fruits and birds of spring
and the direction of an ancient path of fragrant virtues extending to the heavens
inevitably become   forgotten directions

Guo Jinniu (b. 1966, Xishui, Hubei) moved to the Shenzhen-Dongguan area to find employment as a construction worker, dock worker, factory worker, and warehouse worker. He now lives in the Longhua district of Shenzhen. His collection of poetry is called *Going Home on Paper.*

Going Home on Paper

I.

A young boy, one morning before dawn, counts from the first to
the thirteenth floor.
By the time he's done he's on the roof.
He
flies, yes, flies. He can't imitate a bird's movements.
The boy draws a straight line down, fast
as a flash of lightning
only seeing the first half.
The earth, slightly bigger than Longhua district, meets him head-on.
Speed claims the boy; rice claims specks of white.

II.

A mother's tears leap over the tile edge.
This is the thirteenth jump in six months. Those twelve earlier names
are fine just-fallen dust.
The autumn breeze blows all night through the mother's white reeds.
The white ashes, a delicate white, take the train home, unconcerned with
the white of rice, the white of reeds
the white of the mother
the white of the descent of frost
this enormous white, burying a bit of white
like a mother buries a daughter.

III.

My job is installing a suicide guardrail on the thirteenth floor,
for a day's pay,
I force a nail in clockwise bit by bit, as it struggles and resists in
the darkness.
The more force I use, the more dangerous it is.
Rice and fish-fragrant lips, little dimples nourishing two drops of dew.
She still worries.
The garments of autumn
are stripped off day by day.
As for my friend who went home on paper, aside from the rice and your
fiancée,
few mention how in room 701 of this building
you sat on a bunk
eating Dongguan rice noodles.

Bing Ma (b. 1967, Gongan, Hubei) began studying history at Hubei Normal College in 1987 and soon began writing poetry. After graduation, he was sent to teach at the Factory No. 5307 School. After quitting that job in 1993, he bounced between Hainan, Chengdu, Chongqing, Ningbo, and Wuhan. At the end of the 1990s, he moved to Shanghai to work in a drycleaners. In 2001, he was detained, interrogated, and forced to leave the city without cause. His poetry collection is called *Blood in the Snow.*

Cleaning a Wedding Gown

Beating and scrubbing, I use
a hog-bristle brush to scrub in detergent like thin rice gruel

The filth! Grease, lipstick, mud,
sweat-stains and body odor, on the bodice
and skirt, the lower hem and the straps
all over the white and pink sections
it's totally trashed

How can a filthy wedding dress be made spotless?
How can trash become holy and pure? These
are the drycleaners' worries.

May 9-10: Mengzi Road in Shanghai, at the Station under the Custody and Return Program

Numb after squatting, I sit down. At least
the hard wooden floor allows me cross my legs
allows my ass to sit

This ass has supported life's
heaviest weight

To squat or to sit
the two numbing positions replace
the simple wish to go home

When sitting becomes squatting again
the distance between my ass and thighs yet again
sends humiliation and numbness out on further journeys

Hubei Qingwa (b. 1968, Hubei) has been a migrant laborer since 2000, working on construction sites and as a brewer in a state-owned enterprise.

Magpies

I can fall asleep anywhere, but waking up I never hear
the birdsongs of my youth.
The industrial age called people from their homes, in threes and fours
shouldering their cheap woven-plastic bags and dragging them to distant factories.

The factories are already old, but the production line workers
are only in their early twenties.
They are grey magpies, migratory birds, resident birds,
but I'm just a lame duck who gathers withered twigs in winter.

Lame duck, I curse myself, running around China
flying here and there, always looking at tree holes and electricity poles
for a dark nest. It too is a home.
My parents' dilapidated tile-roofed house is my distant home in Hubei.

Cowering, shivering, in the night of middle-age, I feel guilty
that I can't build up my language and country, unable to ease my parents' worries.
These rows of construction materials can't even set my body
in the right place. They crack

and drop.
But I still want to say, I'm my parents' lucky magpie, our country's loyal
propagandist of duty. The others are too.
They come in groups of three or four to the factory doors, they punch their time-clocks.

They punch in at 8 or 8:30am
and spread like poverty over every possible station. They're the ones most
hoping
to bring good news. They are China's lucky magpies,
and they're also China's grief.

Moon's Position in the Factory

1. The Moon and I Take Peeks at Each Other

These days
the moon
has changed its position in the factory

The moon and I reach a secret agreement
during work breaks, like at 9pm
we take peeks at each other

2. The Moon's Professional Life

In terms of its professional life
the moon has its own comprehensive
service orbit

To its direct superior
the moon is pretty, useful from afar
but hard to handle up close

The important thing is that it never gives up

3. The Moon's Promotion

In terms of hiring, promotions, and salary increases,
the moon gets unequal treatment

I see that the moon is just an average performer
under-rested, with hazy eyes
who knows how the moon does it

4. The Moon's Diversity

Sometimes the factory is oddly quiet
the spiders in the nooks and crannies
behave like lovely pregnant women

The moon stands up from the cloud layer
wanting to talk
as you grieve

5. The Moon's Job Description

After that we revised the job description
and we no longer thought about the moon

We were respectful and polite and professional
showing our concern for our cuckolded customers

Trust us
turning a profit—that's what moonlight does

6. The Moon's New Colleagues

After that new colleagues arrived, and at the welcome party
a group of dark faces
were suddenly lit by the moon

The moon followed all of the rules and regulations
never coming late, never leaving early

When the moon is there
everyone is unreasonably happy

7. The Moon's Mistake

The moon likes to wear black and white clothing
the high-level sexually-harassing supervisors
keep nodding, praising the moon's elegance, how enchanting it is

The moon rises over the treetops
to fill in for a few workers

8. Encouraging the Moon

To tell the truth, after that we started training
how to avoid falling behind the moon

We worked extra shifts and hours
and even the boss and his gang of assistants
cheered "Go for it!" "Go for it!" in unison

On the production line, we gave the moon
a new satellite
and we thanked the moon for being a role model

9. The Moon's Attitude Assessment

Given the assessor's bias
it was decided that the moon
performs well only a few nights each month

Seizing the opportunity
we pontificated, joked
and flirted

The rest of the time
we hid the other side of our faces

10. The Moon's Salary

With the increasing dark clouds
the moon can only rely
on an hourly wage

In short, the moon longs
for those blue-sky days
of a monthly salary

11. The Moon's Vacation

Believe that my body can be sweet
and I'll share it with you

But I don't have much money
and neither does the moon

If the moon derails, we'll go off the rails
she should give herself a moon's vacation

12. Complaining to the Moon

Often as I walk through the factory
the moon isn't in front of me
but behind me

Moon, I need to get rid of a problem
but I worry the problem will get rid of me

Moon, loneliness connects us
but you've never said a single word
to me

13. An Uncertain Contract with the Moon

Under the moon, the factory
can't continue

After work, the handwriting gets fuzzier
why not just turn to ash

I will accept myself: under the moon
I have made mistakes

Under the moon, I regret my entire life:
I haven't fulfilled my duties under the moon

Tie Gu (b. 1969, Shuanglong, Sichuan) left school to do farm work in 1984, then began work on a road crew and in a hydroelectric station. In 1995, he moved to Guangdong, where he has worked for nearly twenty years as a construction worker, stonemason, loader, digger, woodworker, and plasterer. He began writing poetry in 2005.

Tower Crane

I've seen many cranes
standing like a powerful eagle
just as a family
must have a sturdy body to support it
but cranes also get old
even when newly painted
the friction of part against part
sounds like an eighty-year old moaning at night
I once watched an old crane
as a worker forced it, with the boss's tacit consent,
to shift heavy loads over and over until one day
it dropped its worn-out head into a news report
my mother was a similar scene
but I never talk details
I wouldn't want my mother up on a platform
waiting for execution like a Paris revolutionary
so every reader's heart
reveals its grief again
I'll never tell my mother up there in heaven
that for over thirty years, I've worked under a crane
just like she squandered her life toiling in the mud

Barber

A canvas bag, a kettle, a washbasin,
a folding chair. The seventy year old with a lame leg
often turns up in the trees near the Imperial Mall,
he's not creative, it's always crew cut, shaved head, bowl cut
but he's good at shaving, so every time I feel down
I go to him for a shave, and by now it's like we know each other,
and though we've never talked, from the sound
of his razor I know his mood
and he can tell my troubles from how much energy I have.
On September 30, my boss gave me my pay
and said there was no more work, he told me to go home and rest
he'd tell us when there was a new project. Before I left
I checked four different places to find
the old man, who to my surprise had set up in the woods behind the
    police station,
but it makes sense, the more dangerous the place the safer it is
and just as usual, I closed my eyes and leaned back in the chair,
the old man's razor was sharpened on a scrap of leather as always
but that harsh sound seemed less carefree and easy
and more like the fury of preparing for battle,
when his five fingers supported my head
I felt he was enjoying the sensation of throttling an enemy's throat
the knife's edge was like drumbeats and battle flags and cavalry crossing
    the earth
and as it swept over my throat, I had a faint sense of anticipation
and I could tell that he also felt an excited pity

Tang Yihong (b. 1970, Yilong, Sichuan) left for Shenyang to work in construction before graduating from middle school. In 1994, he began working in a shoe factory in Guangzhou. He then went back to construction work, living in places like Shenzhen, Dongguan, Foshan, and Beijing. The unstable lifestyle interrupted his poetry writing for many years, until he began work in a shoe factory in Wenzhou in 2004 and picked up his pen again.

Returning Home Backwards

Returning from Beijing to Shenzhen, from Dongguan
to Hangzhou, from Changshu to Ningbo
from Wenzhou to Chengdu, returning to the earth and plants
to the fragrance of grain, home is still
very far away, it's a pair of lost straw sandals
return and return, return from the factories
return from machines, return from tears,
return from forty back to thirty
to twenty, to ten. . .home is still
very far, it's a pair of lost straw sandals
return and return, facing the future
return to your mother's body—and there
there's no glory or dishonor, no difference between rich and poor
no separation between city and country. There are no tears
and everyone you meet is family

It Seems I'm Really His Father

When I went home one time, my son
was playing with the neighbor's kid
when he saw me he hid behind my mother's body
sticking his fingers in his mouth, sucking on them
as he peeked out, quietly, timidly
sizing me up, as though I weren't his father
but the neighbor's kid was excited
not knowing what to do with himself, singing for a bit
then dancing, then riding a kitchen stool
flying about shouting, circling my courtyard
running one lap then another, wanting to get close to me
until it was dark and he still didn't want to go home
so it seems I'm really his father

Hide That Uniform Away

The uniform is gray
and I want to hide it
the gray of tearstains and sweat-stains
glue odor, machine oil odor, the odor of grievances
homesickness in the seams
I want to hide all that too
it's twenty years old, the time I've spent in the factory
I'll hide those twenty years
they're so big, they once bound me
like binding a soundless cicada
that's trembling all over
I'll hide the trembling
hide it, hide it all
take its gray color, and
all the diligent work and my mute self
the others who made me mute
and hide it all away in the deepest place
hide it where no one can find it
I'm afraid I'll drag it out
from deep in my memory
so it can make me suffer again
so it can wound me

Mixer

It's already rusty and mottled
and the patches made with a welding torch
have aged even more, layered up and battered
its birthplace and model are blurry
but I know its functions—
tell it to spin, it spins
tell it to stop, it stops
it doesn't belong to itself
it belongs to the construction site, the factory, the assembly line
to this gloomy life and reality
and even the rust on its body
will be beaten off with a heavy hammer
it turns and thirty years pass like a single day
it gobbles down life's gravel, scrap paper, rubber pellets
and waste, and spits out a moonlike
religion and its own organs
its voice is gravelly
its teeth are loose like those returning home, the revolving driving belt
has just been changed, it's gone from an original product
to a motley assemblage. I still miss
its distorted face, and its inner
thundering and pain
don't belong to it either

Tear-filled Paradise

I lived there for half a year. I knew their business like the back of my hand,
even the things that can't be talked about. It's the fate of working couples
born in rooster years. Scrabbling for meals in construction sites, bus
    stations, wharfs, garbage dumps
or assembly lines, using blood and sweat to take care of parents, bring up
    children, feed
and clothe themselves, pay the water and electricity bills, set up temporary
    residence, have sex just like you do
but, when you're in your bed or someone else's, or in bar or club
crying out desperately with joy, near death, they're still smoking cheap
    cigarettes,
using the cheapest menstrual pads, living in the crudest apartments
as mute couples.

In that place stripped bare of clothes and objects
are many bodies and souls. Many rooms separated by plywood or by paper
and many rickety beds. Many sheets and cheap woven-plastic bags like
    fig-leaves
blown up by the wind so the moon can steal a peek. Beaten by life during
    the day
only able to return at night, treating their wounds with flames
they have to seek a bit of leftover happiness with their bodies
and their bodies are a tear-filled paradise

There, I never heard singing, only
an exploratory creaking and squeaking of cots on the other side of the
    paper at night
and getting the hint, other beds start to creak, one at first
then two, then many, all creaking very cautiously
like a weak chorus. I trust that among them, someone
is tightly covering his mouth. During the day no one cries in pain, and no
    one dares cry out
with their bit of pleasure at night. No one dares cry out.
So many bodies and souls hide themselves like thieves in the night

and they're often dragged out from the nighttime's smidgen
of pleasure. Bare-chested, they huddle
in rows under the eaves to accept interrogation. Interrogate
their identity as couples of temporary workers, working couples, couples
 who've been worked.

Wastewater ditches. Garbage dumps. Darkness and damp. Advertisements
 for itinerant doctors.
Impotent and desolate, cold words, blotted-out sky, it all makes people feel
that's who they are. Some of them must be that way. I often hear
the Zhangs fighting, or the Lis fighting. Mostly about money
the other thing no one can talk about.

November 8, Beside Su Xiaoxiao's Grave

Many lean in close to her
to take photos, as though leaning in close to their own woman
I also take a photograph
on that five hundred year old pink bed
she sleeps sweetly
I don't dare wake her, worried she'll open her mouth and say—
husband, silver coins.
Today prices are rising, and her status would surely rise with the tide
a working stiff who can't even make bus fair
I'd never get that much money
the most important thing is that when we take a photo together,
          I suddenly feel
I'm going behind the back of my assembly-line wife
and having an affair
she was a famous courtesan of the south
and when I think of the others
I take my unfair wages and my bus fare back home
and blow it all at a cleavage-filled 'salon'
I righteously stand up straight—
What's there to fear? It's just a photo with the dead

Chen Nianxi (b. 1970, Zhoufeng, Shaanxi) has a middle school education. He was a demolitions worker in coalmines for fifteen years.

Meaning

The three of us, Old Chen, Old Li, and Little Song
come from Shaanxi, Sichuan, and Shandong
we work in demolitions
brought together
not by loyalty or friendship
and definitely not by fate

Each day
we drill holes, pack powder, blast, eat, sleep
and feel our lives are meaningless
a meal of braised pork every three days and an explosion every day
give our lives the most meaning

Once
we got drunk
and Little Song sang an old Shandong tale
in his rough loud voice, and the drums and clanging
and the ancient drama
brought back the hero Wu Song for a while
Old Li suddenly started to cry
he said, I'm sorry Little Qin,
and said it and said it until he started to laugh
he laughed and said
if a man falls in love once in his life
he isn't poor
finally I belted out the Shaanxi opera "The Chen Shimei Case"
and got so angry

I cut down Chen's concubine myself
afterwards, we all said
that we'd drunk back half a lifetime's meaning

The year before last
Little Song was diagnosed with silicosis
the day he died
his wife used his last month's salary
to hire the town's best band
to play Wu Song's music to send him off

Last year
Old Li's leg was taken by a capstone
and the Chengdu mahjongg stalls
gained
a single-legged crane

Today, I'm still in the mines
I drill holes, pack powder, blast, eat, sleep
my two new assistants are children
their slang and games
mean nothing to me
the daily braised pork and explosions
have long since been meaningless
into middle age, I don't know
whether I'll ever
find a bit of meaning in my life

The east wind picks up
meaning is blown in
and meaning is blown away
blown and blown
until all is blown to dust

Demolitions Mark

Daybreak and my head feels like it's exploding
this is the gift of a mechanized society
it isn't the fault of steel
it's that my nerves have grown old and feeble

I don't often dare look at my life
it's hard and metallic black
angled like a pickaxe
when the rocks are hit they will bleed

I spend my middle age five kilometers inside mountains
I explode the rocks layer by layer
to put my life back together

My humble family
is far away at the foot of Mt. Shang
they're sick and their bodies are covered in dust
whatever is taken from my life
extends the tunnel of their old age

My body carries three tons of dynamite
and they are the fuse

Last night
I exploded like the rocks

Son

Son,
we haven't seen each other for so long
the dream I had last night of holding you
hangs with the dew
at the head of the bed

You're twenty miles from home at school
I'm two thousand miles from home on a barren hill
your mother
a woman of forty-eight
is bound by the crops
on the rainy fields

The three of us
are like three legs
propping up a table called family
son, this separation of thousands of miles of mountains
is just the way things are

Life isn't fairytales and cartoons
son
we're being whipped on by three different whips
your dad is tired
each step is only three inches wide
and three inches take a year
son, use your math to calculate
how far your dad can go

You say your mother is a peony
this spring
the peony has been blooming for years
its leaves have fallen and its fragrance faded
no one can halt the steady march of autumn
son

your mother is a kernel of corn
born as maize and returned to maize
and all that can be taken away
is an empty stalk

Son
your clear gaze
sees through words and numbers
sees through the Transformers
but it can't see the reality
I want you to put down your books and look at the world
but I fear you would really see it

Yang Sai and Yang Zai

The place I work is called Yang Sai
a narrow gully on the southern slope of the Xiqinling mountains
there's no one named Yang and there's no Sai encampment
what brought us there was a vein of gold

Our thoughts, our love and hate and revenge
are all expressed in explosives, it tells of our
poverty and homelessness, our distance that leads to divorce
it tells that some are fated to be rich or poor and it's always been that way
in front of the explosives is death
behind them is life
our work is like the assassin trying to kill the Qin emperor

In our group is a guy named Yang Zai
a descendent of the secret society from the river's west bank
he's got an appetite for food and liquor, and can take a lot of hardship
the locust trees above our heads and eight generations of fallen oak leaves
are prolific as some writers

Each day I tuck my clothes in and tighten my belt
my miner's lamp lights my dark future
I diagnose the mineral vein
then determine the exact spot to drop the blade
like a doctor diagnosing the prime minister of Zhou
if I make the slightest mistake or hesitate
we will all suffer, young and old

The eight-hectometer deep shafts form a huge labyrinth
like the Tiger-head Fortress and the imperial tombs
at the bottom of one of the shafts, I once saw a group of robbers
who'd been dropped by the poisonous gases
their bodies were so still they looked like a pile of ore
their wives and children came out of their pockets in photographs
to gently shut their eyes

In September of 2011 I left Yang Sai and Yang Zai
and never went back
I've heard they built a tavern in the eastern valley
while the flags of the dead crowd the western slopes
I heard that one day Yang Zai ran too fast and got ahead of the explosives
and ran into a cloud of smoke
his wife sent me a few texts from her home on the west riverbank
saying night after night someone cries in the woods behind their house
I never answered

The past few years   it rarely snows on Mt. Shangluo
I don't know if Yang Sai and the west riverbank
are the same or not
the snow is gone   but winter is still here

Li Shangge (b. 1970, Nanchong, Sichuan) worked as a manual laborer around Guangdong for seven years before getting various jobs as a manager, reporter, editor, and curator.

Temporary Worker

> The industrial history of China from the 1980s up until today is the bloody history of the temporary worker; it is also a chaotic, ugly industrial history that will influence the world. —Inscription

Year follows on year, and what year are we in tonight? Brothers and sisters
let us awaken, let us touch life's numbness and pain
and humiliation. Let God remove all the suffering bodies from
the enormous factories. Out from the mighty current of industry,
from the hypocritical faces, from the foul grease and dirt, remove
our tubercular bodies, and let the fierce sun scorch us again—
the corroded souls and indifferent black blood. Be ruthless!
Let us touch our own mute hearts and bones! Brothers and sisters,
let us awaken, leave behind our work and illnesses for the moment, leave
behind steel, iron, copper, aluminum, and silver all soaked in sweat
and menstrual blood, leave behind the machines, noise, work
orders, punishment, layoffs and unconcerned eyes, and cry
on a hill where lychee trees bloom, in your distant hometowns,
calling for your mother and father, your wives, the village elders
and townsmen. Let our hearts cross the slow and desolate
railroad tracks of the south, returning to hollow villages a thousand li away—
there, our boys have already been born with pure
testicles, running through the open prairies. And our daughters,
who still suffer the pains of menstruation…Let us apologize, ashamed!
And let our compassionate hearts speak of love: give us
innocent sons and daughters. Remember their melancholy
lonely childhoods, their rough and hopeless upbringing. Let

us cry on those broad open prairies: for our relatives cultivating
the fields by lamplight, for those shadows growing gradually old
in the fields of our hometowns, for the kind earth and rainwater,
the beasts and grains, for the constant asthma and moaning under
the withered chinaberry trees—the distracted and dismal
mourning of loved ones! Let us mourn for the wilderness now
filled with the odor of pesticides: when sparrows die in droves,
and the crows fly away in flocks, let us stand in silent tribute
for our dear ones who were felled by potassium chloride and
ammonium bicarbonate. Pay respects. Let us always give tribute!
And for the last fertile fields, for the bugle that calls to work and
each day grows weaker, let us close our eyes: for our beloved
dead plow oxen, our women, houses, land. When farmers have no
land left to plant and poverty becomes a fear that cannot
be dispelled from the villages, let us cry bitterly:
for the desolation ravaging the faces of our loved ones,
for those children who are undernourished or forced to leave
school. For those hungry children holding their crudely made
bowls! Let us apologize, ashamed: those pale lips and dazed
pupils, prematurely carved with life's despair and hatred. Yes,
when they grow up and leave home, our villages lose their
love songs. Our homes are no longer homes full of poetry
and wild flowers and love! Our villages are no longer simple,
beautiful and clean! Ah, the destitute villages quietly die,
and nothing is left of their era. Let us be sad: for the prayers
of our tearful far-flung loved ones, wish them well, in
unfamiliar places, wish them a bright future. As they flee,
ceaselessly wandering—this is our common unavoidable fate!
As the trains thunder past our hometowns' persimmon trees,
let us remember those pained eyes, those countless waving
hands outside the windows. Let us remember the stations,
wharfs, harbors, snowflakes, chaotic crowds. This is the
industrial south, the freshest and most tragic act. Remember
their bitter weeping and shouts! As the trains pierce the fields'
tranquility, the snow falls on those seeing others off—oh! our dear ones
are scattered and night has already fallen. To our dear ones coughing
up black blood under the eaves, pick up your old occupations!

To those with their heads to the yellow mud and backs to the sky,
complete your fate entwined with the earth. The rural problem,
the rural population problem, the agricultural problem, continue
to be problems only halfheartedly addressed. As bulldozers push
into the countryside, let us listen attentively to the earth cursing
the insatiable cities. The howls of the villages cannot overpower
the pile driver's low roar...Brothers and sisters, let us remember
our dear ones with their blue veins protruding under the scorching
sun. They love the earth beneath their feet, and cannot escape
that same impoverished fate of the earth. As farmers load grain
into barns, how many people come to the end of their lives on the
desolate ground? As they die one by one, let us cry for our dear
ones who struggle under medicine and cotton swabs. Let us remember
their kindness and love and sorrows, their loneliness and darkness
and resolve. As they die in widespread poverty, incurable,
let us engrave them on our minds, and gnash our teeth. In the
trumpet of night, snow descends, and let us hold our funeral processions
and burials. And as our dear ones depart from this abnormal
agriculture, may death give them a kind of eternal consolation,
and in the distant heavens, may the gods bestow peace upon them.
Brothers and sisters, let us wipe away our sweat and tears, and use
our hoarse singing to recall those long-gone countryside songs,
let deathly still hearts come back to life—and see those diminishing
great rivers: the Yangtze, the Yellow, the Pearl, the Huai, the Min,
the Xiang, the Luan, the Jialing...They still reverberate day and night,
shouting, roaring, surging, for every single desperate unmoored life.

Lizi (b. 1970, Zhaoyang, Liaoning) worked in a brickyard in her hometown for three years after middle school. In 1992, she moved south to Zhejiang, working in a workshop that made plumbing fittings, and on assembly lines assembling refrigeration parts and manufacturing enamel wire. She is now the head editor of a company's internal publication. She began writing poetry in 2002, and she is the author of the collection *A Rain of Poems at Midnight*, and a collaborative book-length piece of reportage, *Rays of Gold.*

Close as Fingers

On the assembly line, ten fingers dance
close to the widgets
far from the worker's heart
if the moon can soothe the night tonight
her ten fingers will continue to dance
and she might manage to forget
the unceasing circling pain

Who knew that ten fingers could flower
into callouses, that over and over they work
the assembly line's copper widgets and iron widgets
but still the lines of her palms
carry a faint silken scent

The callous blossoms drop into dreams
and start to savor a relationship as close as fingers
she starts calling and calling for her loved ones
faraway lamps light up and then darken again
the road is like an assembly line, stretching out into the distance

Working the Nightshift

Now, lifting their heads they can't see the moon
and the abstracted morning glories
the women walk quietly on the nightshift
and under their feet is no tangible dew

That breath, those nervous twitches
those bodies that can't tell if it's night or day
run through turbid memories

What can dilute this labor
and ferry them back toward home
what if there were a faint summons
that they could feel, a pair of hands
gently opening a red lacquered door

Li Shougang (b. 1971, Yunyang, Chongqing) began working in a brickyard in Hubei in 1989. In 1992, he started work as a coal miner in Wuda, Inner Mongolia, where he witnessed several colleagues die in a mine collapse. In 1993, while working in a car garage, he lost control of a high-powered punch press and lost four fingers on his left hand. His poetry collections are *Worker's Schedule* and *Between City and Country.*

1992: Wuda, Inner Mongolia

When the wind comes in it kicks up my matted hair
the grit the wind carries
weeps in the eyes
and won't come out
I'm hurrying from the Wuda New Area
to my job in the black coal mine
the journey between them is an afternoon's
distance of foot and leg

What I find in the mine is only darkness
and fear
the hardhat on my head
plays its role
between the gas and the air vents
my breath is timid

My coworker's screams
are drowned in the sound of a collapsing wall
I see on his pain-distorted face
a layer of coal ash
peeling off

1993: Repair Shop in Jiangkou

Pressure, extension, rending
sounds of metal crushing metal
through each day of 1993
I was tethered to memories of that evening
fingers are so vulnerable
with a momentary slip of attention at the punch press
the flesh was mutilated
moaning was useless
I had to face the pain
like I faced my damaged left hand
holding onto my heart

An Shiliu (b. 1972, Shiliu Village, Guangxi) began writing at the end of the 1980s. In 1993, he left for Shenzhen to work as a printer, warehouse manager, editor, advertisement writer, and screenplay writer. He is the author of the poetry and essay collections *Uneasy, My Geography of Shenzhen, Bubbles,* and *An Ordinary Day in the Songzhuang Artists' Village.*

Spring Festival: Train

The trains run for a year across the belly of the earth
ruining its digestion
we saved up a year of drudgery and longing
forced to run even when sick like the train
only one toppled railing remains on the earth
crossing over this indelible sequence
that can barely complete last year's sunlight

It's snowed for a month, destroying a year of roads
the earth buried its surface, and mankind returns home defeated
how long will we be delayed by the cold year-end winds
the train tracks are like a worn-out watchband
that can never quite affix
the time of arrival to the wrist
the last schedule of the year
can't be entrusted to itself

The Spring Festival is never late, the train accelerates again and again
the high-speed train's improving temper
means ticket prices can't be used as an excuse anymore
there are frequent freezing announcements of slowed speed
and scalpers who defeat the system of names on tickets
the land's hard narrow spine
can't even carry a thin train ticket

how can we make it to next spring
the sunlight is running hard, like us year after year

Xie Xiangnan (b. 1974, Leiyang Village, Hunan) has planted rice and raised pigs, fish, and cattle. He moved to Shenzhen and started writing poetry in 1993. He has worked as a construction worker and in a toy factory, hardware factory, paper mill, electronics factory, and state-run enterprise. In 2003, he began working as a reporter and editor at the *Southern Metropolis Daily*. His poetry collections include *Docker at Midnight* and *Allergy.*

Breath

The fans are silent
the towels are silent
the metal mugs and toothbrushes are silent
the neighboring bed gives a hint of Zhang Xueyou
the bags are silent
the scattered shirts and pants are silent
the green slippers and red plastic buckets are silent
I want to write a poem so I light a cigarette
on the wall is a smiling transparent girl
chewed chewing gum
and the blood of slaughtered mosquitoes

This is room 106 of the male dormitory at the hardware factory
it's eighteen days from the Spring Festival
                    the mild season
          it's nine-thirty
                    on a Sunday evening

The guy in bunk 1 went to get noodles
the guy in bunk 2 is out repairing watches
the guy in bunk 3 is on a date
the guy in bunk 4 is "guarding" the TV at the dormitory entrance
the guy in bunk 5 has tears in his eyes from cigarette smoke

the guy in bunk 6 is the perpetually drunk Zhang Xueyou
the guy in bunk 7 is talking to another guy from Shaanxi
the guy in bunk 8   is gone
there used to be   three other men here
                    who now are nowhere to be found

Work Accident Joint Investigative Report

Gong Zhonghui
Female
20 years old
From Ji'an, Jiangxi
Work Number: z0264
Department: Plastics
Type of Work: Die cutting machine
Entered Factory: 08.24.1997

In the process of cutting plastic, the product did not appear, the safety door did not open
the hand entered from the side to release
the product. The hand
touched
the safety door
and as it shut
it applied pressure
to the middle and ring fingers
at the second joint of the middle finger and first joint of the ring finger
which is considered a "transgression of factory safety operating procedures"

People reported
her hands were often burnt to blisters by the machine
people reported
she'd been working continuously for twelve hours
people reported after it happened   she
didn't cry   and didn't
scream   she just grabbed her finger
and left

When it happened   no one
was there   to see it

On Sunday, We Gather in the Post Office

The post office is closest to home
closest to my father's stomach problems
closest to my brother's school

on Sunday, we gather in the post office
lining up in front of money orders of a month of sweat
listening hard and talking hard

walking into a phone booth and the source of the sound
we can't bear to put our tears and pain into our letters
to dispel all the happiness and curiosity, so on a Sunday

we send along a holiday to aging ears
or a child's expectant eyes. A present
going into the mailbox after insistent urgings

Sunday, we gather in the post office
stranger with stranger, one local accent with another
and on a piece of white paper, the blank spaces of years—

You Have to Sit Down and Get Used to Such Sounds

You have to sit down and get used to such sounds
get used to different qualities of amps
people shouting   electric synthesizers
accompaniment   announcements   people yelling at the stage
the sound of iron   of cutting
gears   and their spinning   their kinetic friction
the construction site's   humming wires
two people together   are separated by the sound
of a kind of distance   a solid sound
an earsplitting sound

You have to sit down and get used to such sounds
a turning lock   the sound of a computer
the sound of dust falling
the sound of dark colors
a heart's beat
felt and repeated endlessly
this kind of sound
fills and envelopes you   forces you to lie down
standing and fidgeting   it empties you out
not knowing its name   not able to say why
this kind of sound   a sound as turbid and enormous as water

You have to sit down and get used to such sounds
like getting used to sitting down
with no one around you   and no one will ever come

Orders of the Front Lines

My finest five years went into the input feeder of a machine
I watched those five youthful years come out of the machine's
asshole—each formed into an elliptical plastic toy,
slippery, sometimes orange,
sometimes bright red and green eggshells.
(I've heard they're shipped to America, shipped
to Western Europe as Christmas toys, sold one after another
to blue-eyed children.....)

The puffing machine spouts green smoke
biting into my whimpering fervor with a teeth-grinding rhythm
the luster of engine oil could be a mirror to get dressed in
and so for five years the mosquitoes don't dare frequent
my body, the butcher shop of my hot unhurried blood

In the busiest production season, the boss and his
wife, those two lovers, each come to the workshop
to walk around and watch, sometimes bringing two bags
of dried fish, to stuff into the mouths of my brothers and sisters

.....they're clever, they often decide
to appear behind me when I'm most anxious
making me act like that machine spouting smoke, making me
stand there obediently. And the back-flowing urine
circles around into tonight.....

The Busy Crowds Congeal

Six o'clock, and I'm not prepared
the dawn is impatient, the windowsill seems crude
the guy frying strips of dough masters the fryer's calm
everything changes quickly, the dough turns golden

Six o'clock, and I'm not prepared
the sun strips the ocean of its white nightgown
it puts on jeans, accentuating its lines
those who've left home are seduced, they forget to say goodbye to their
families

Retreating from the nightshift to seek their own schedules
their bodies shout and yield
to the sounds that accompany the city's elevated train
—entering sleep……

Let's Have More Poets Like Xie Xiangnan

Tell it to the world
don't just leave it in a drawer
or merely give names to cockroaches

The leaves begin to yellow
in the scene where the streets mate
winter seizes the autumn's hair
entering the body
of the world from behind

Let's have more
more poets like Xie Xiangnan
they don't come from the storm clouds above
but from the belly of the earth
from those workers just stopping for the day
carrying shovels and hammers, from that sloppily dressed
group of men

Listening to a Song on an Endless Train Ride

Put down your sickle
put down your hoe
leave your sons
and leave your mothers
sell your pigs and sheep
abandon your land
separate from your wife
we're going into the city

We're going into the city
we want to go to the city
what will we do in the city
we'll see when we get there

Guangzhou Train Station, March 1996

I remember the painting "Liberty Leading the People,"
a fairly safe picture, it appeared in our middle school history book
along with "Lenin on the Rostrum," in which people gather below the stage
and raise up their weapons. I seem to remember hearing a sound leaping
from the page—
there was a huge crowd at the Guangzhou train station in March 1996 too
the bags piled on the square were like packages of explosives
and I almost imagined the digital clock towering overhead
was our beloved Lenin. Two foreign men in suits stood
beside a sign, an advertisement for American cigarettes
and in March 1996, I was still a kid from the country who didn't smoke
pushed off the train by the flow of people, I was like a log
just pulled out of the forest. The earth and sky had already changed
a five-kuai meal could only fill up one corner of my stomach
and people kept bumping into me—brushing past
with the same face, like uncontrollable revolutionary fever
an old man in an armband had caught a woman and was going to fine her
while girls loitered in the courtyard and laid out their wares in the night
fruit and motor scooters, newsstands and scalpers flashed past my eyes
how many people were there? Or maybe it was just me: waiting
for "Beloved Lenin" to open a breach in time
to take the unfamiliar clothing—and put it on like a pro.

Girls Buried in Shenzhen

Xiantao Chongqing Changsha Xinxing Ningbo Anhui Henan
you're from different places
born somewhere else
but you all happened to come to this place
to the bougainvillea kapoks lychees ravenala verbena lemon eucalyptus
from the places where you grew up, to another
place to live

It seems no one knew how you lived
or how you felt when you came to this land
and now you have fixed smiles
unmoving on the gravestones

Your vibrant bodies once traversed the city's lanes
in the clothing factories toy factories electrical workshops behind
counters in offices
you worked all day and then did overtime
in the stairwells of the shantytowns, you passionately
kissed your lovers
and after a nightshift went to the street markets to use candy or something
spicy
to soothe your lonely stomachs
and now the sound by your ears is still the clamor of constructions sites
the sound of tires rolling past

Strands of pearls roll into different days and nights
youth ends abruptly
and the tidelines end at the city meters
now passion has nothing to do with you
maybe your ideal is to blur yourself into your own shadows
and do you still hold secrets

The city lights stare down at your loved ones
that's when you truly become subtropical plants

on the periphery of the city
with the evening dew as your companion
perhaps you'll still come down into the city sky for a stroll
but this city already doesn't know you
and that white skirt, now that it's been rinsed three times
no longer gives off the stink of sweat

Production, in the Middle of Production, Is Soaked by Production

1.

With my lungs tested by autumn
the dust I encountered was definite
I wasn't floating
I was in the middle of production

I produced black and made white
and crawled into the cracks between black-white distinctions
I was in the middle of production
soaked by the moisture of production

I produced a table
the table held up the snowstorm for me
I made a bed
the bed installed a spring inside me
I raised a newspaper
the newspaper was eloquent and cheerless
I made a road public
and the umbrellas on the road were heartbroken

2.

My face tightens
and I have to rub my eyes
it hurts
there's grit in them

Where's the grit from
tell me
where's the grit from
tell me
how can the grit be so large

tell me
the grit in my eyes
in my throat
in my bile
how long will it stay there

3.

Grit carried in by wind
blocks the season
burns out blood
a tree's panting
a plot of land's covering of leaves

I'm not like the plants
a mighty army of dust gallops through my chest
a magnificent wind
scrubs the trees clean
the lungs of this era
are crushed like asbestos

4.

In links
by deep links
deeper and deeper links
then, I'm baffled by the light
I'm a railroad tie under the light
I lie across an invisible dance
approaching an uncontrollable winter night
I'm inlayed in fire
still burning with fever, still producing

This is a rectangular dream
which inevitably brings forth a rectangular waiting
a floating country can't pillow a broken dream
and I've never dared say goodnight to this enormous world

5.

The world's factories cover the nightshift
the faces more wrinkled the more they're rubbed
a pile of mouths, partly parched
a row of footprints, trampling other bodies, scratching
each other painfully. She lifts her hands, touches the heart of the night,
and my heart
has been labeled
a riddle
Saturday has been labeled an occupational injury

6.

Finally, soaked lungs can rest
production is still the noise of the advance guard, accompanying
a ringing in the ears. The motor is inflamed
and I want to let it stop, this drop of water's breathing
can't moisten parched cracked lips, and I want to let it stop
its leaden breathing, drooping like the loudspeakers
dark substances are electric currents rushing forward
the heaviness makes its dam-breaking body
reassemble like the earth's crust

7.

I have a few withered branches
I have a frozen burning

In my ice is the tongue
of hidden time, allergenic enzymes

I have sleepless dandruff
that was lost on the hard road

When I lightly touch my own hair
passing by the truncated street of midnight

I discuss paper airplane wings
with someone, some fat guy
along with his fear

Ni Wen (b. 1974, outside Chongqing) left school in 1993 to work in a coal mine. He also worked in demolitions and construction. In 1998, he began to work on the assembly line in a machine factory in Chongqing. He now works repairing power-generating equipment. He began writing poetry in 2002.

Filling Out Job Applications

The name blank is easy to fill, each time there's no need to think about it
I can write in
the color of mud that my parents used for my name
gender is simple, I'm clear about that
as for ethnicity, I've never been able to prove it
I'm only what my residence permit says I am
then on to the crucial school record
and my pen feels embarrassed, since I have no proof
I've gone to school at all. The red booklet saying I finished a correspondence
class
wasn't officially approved, while my date of birth
can only match the mistake on my ID card
that's the only approved way to do it, a legal citizen
married, with nothing political, no profession to speak of,
who's hit bottom, a home address can be filled out, but there's no way of
getting in touch
the office phone is someone else's, the home phone is a blank
from some month and year to some other month and year, working or
studying
that's all easy to say, in '92 I started working at a brickyard in Hebei
in '93 I demolished old houses in Shanghai, in '98 I worked on an assembly
line in Chongqing
it could be called work or study, the posts and positions
can be stated calmly, as for family members

start with my parents and move to my wife, all dressed in the same colors
of farmers, the countryside, agricultural work
in the column for recommenders, I can't think of anyone
so I recommend myself

Tao Tiancai (b. 1977, Yibin, Sichuan) has worked in Dongguan and now lives in Fuzhou. He worked as a docker for two years, before taking jobs in a brewery, plastics factory, and shoe factory. He has also worked as a business manager, an art designer, and an editor. His poetry collection is called *Three Questions.*

Chitchat

Our third kid, what a fuckup.
He's worked for years, how can he still be broke?
Hasn't brought a single penny home;
hasn't gotten a single girl.....

"Yesterday we were drinking at a wedding, and your aunt said:
'Didn't your youngest just come back?
Why doesn't he come over? His cousin
wants to go job-hunting with him! Her bags are already packed.'"

"I'm not pulling your leg. If you want to talk women,
I've always said you could find one in a porta-potty!"
Worried, what would I be worried about? I'm not worried.
What do you mean nervous? I'm not nervous.

Are you for real? You think I'm being serious,
I'd abandon my parents without a second thought?
No way! No matter what, I know this:
these muscles didn't come spending all day in bed.

The weather's so dry you have to dig holes by the river to get water;
if the sow had a litter of three, two would drop dead,
God has no conscience. My old man wrote me a letter:
Son, we're getting old so we can't even toss and turn in bed....

Sun Haitao (b. 1978, Shaoyang, Hunan) was a soldier for five years and then moved to Dongguan in 2002 to work as a security guard, a grinding machine operator, and a technician in a print shop. He now works for the Dongguan Cultural Center.

Employment ID

The light affixes. The paper has yellowed
away an inch of the youth in the photograph
the only thing worth pondering is the stupid childish smile
back then, it covered up so much misery

The light turns. Reproduced days and nights
for a decade, without names and jobs
a man shrinks to four Arabic numerals
to be ordered around in the workshop

The light passes. The blood and sweat or glory and honors—
let it all go to hell
a man steps forward on the ice
my thirty years face into a windstorm for yet another beginning

Machine Documentation

—During the 2008 economic crisis

Covered by twilight the huge cooling chunk of iron
gives off a darkening silence. Maybe it makes us think
of midnight with its numb motions
looking out from the workshop, the stars are lifting
the vastness of the southern night sky
just as we lift the uncertainties of the future
we crouch at the intersection to smoke, and complain
about these days of treading on thin ice

Crossing the print shop's color lab to that dark window
we can go beyond the security walls all the way to the mountains
whose slopes are covered with weeds and wild flowers and bushes……
most of which we couldn't name
as the wind blows past, we gaze up at the vast sky
and the distant phosphorescent lights twinkling there—
it seems nothing else can make us feel so calm

Someone will lift an old fashioned German printer
which is on its last legs. It's from a time we endured together
a night road we will return on
we just quietly sit at the frigid machines
quietly waiting, watching the night
gradually disperse from the sky's broad burial clothes

Chen Caifeng (b. 1979, Zaoyang, Hubei) began writing poetry in 1999. After graduating from middle school, he went south to work in Guangdong as a desolderer and maker of plug-in components in an electronics factory, and then as a materials feeder and molder in a plastics factory. He currently works as a machinist.

The Women

In the workshop, in the deep night, their eyes are bloodshot
and their tired gazes hover in the air

Those hands are busy and rough. Rigid movements, pursued and hurried on
by product after product. Between talk, that faint smile
under the fluorescent lights along the assembly line,
silences day and brings night back to life

Let the hollow sounds of the worms in their bellies overcome
the roar of the machines; let them overcome the cold of the night coming on
someone is thinking of village roads, the foxtail
has scattered its seeds in the middle of the roads

And the moment the sky lightens
they do it all again: take inventory, pack crates, load up the warehouse....

Under Fluorescent Lights

The rotary files polished by burrs
follow a series of stiff motions
under the fluorescent lights, frantically
seeking out any possible happiness

The plastic molding machine grabs the assembly line by the throat
lets the light play the madman
one by one the dust's hands
ache, go numb, and even malfunctions

are negligible, unremarkable
in the factory, in the clamor of the machines, in the hidden places of light
one place buried under another

It's only the panic implanted into the body, again
oppressed by fear, admonishing oneself:
behind me is my child, my mother, my father

Plastic Molding Factory

1.

Accidentally dropped into the mountains, no echo to be found

More than a thousand tons of plastic molding machines live in half a
square kilometer, and at noon the mechanical arm
practices its stroll in the air, a group of ants frantically
works the assembly line, groups of plastic pellets
hurry to the firing, high temperatures, extrusion

On the worktable is a small blade, tape,
tape dispensers, production labels, and in the end no one knows where it
all goes

2.

Each product in the hand
is turned over into a finished product

Black ones, white ones, looking at the stars outside
standard operating procedures and packing instructions flicker
the small blade in the hand hooks into the return key
and pain flows out

This sound finds no echo, in the workshop
everyone minds his own business, and no one knows
how many times these soaked uniforms have been dried

3.

Open the door, close the door;
it's all automatic, semiautomatic
rotary files, burrs
disbonding, trapped air.......

If you're not careful, you'll leak out too
a visitor says, it's rough when you touch it; make it better
in the deathly pale of the overhead light, the worktable
is like a stage, my hands and feet dance
rifling through things, seeking out the right moment to appear on stage

4.

The plastic molding machine repeats
the mechanical arms repeat
we repeat adding materials, setting the molds, adjusting the machine

Everything is repeated, we are repeated
night and day take over for each other, is it night or is it day
no one knows, nothing is known

5.

Perhaps the flow of a product
can testify to a worker's dream

Stooping to pick up a lost plastic product
he seems as heavy as a million pounds
my eyes are so tired they won't open

I know what he wants to say and do
he's just like the plastic molding machine
risking life and limb, each wave higher than the next
the orange daybreak climbs up slowly outside
like a silent father standing nearby

6.

He's delivered from oppression at dawn or dusk
cheap smokes, discount liquor, when he gets off work
and goes through the door he thinks, doesn't stop thinking
and thinking, thinking until he sleeps

and dreams of his mother, his home in a lovely mountain village
where he sometimes even laughs, there among those huge mountains

Li Zuofu (b. 1979, Xingguo, Jiangxi) has worked as a carpenter's helper, a miner, and a logger. Living in Shenzhen from 1999 to 2005, he worked his way up from the assembly line to positions as a repairman, a quality control assistant, and a production technician. He now works as a quality control manager.

A Bowl

An unfamiliar place.
Stuffed in like dumpling fillings: Houjie, Daoyao, Changping, Dalang,
Huangjiang, Liaobu.
Stuffed into two envelopes: one to my Zhanjiang relatives, one to my
Jiangmen friends, a hasty pyramid scheme.
Carsick all the way to Siqian, flat broke and brainwashed.
I returned to that unfamiliar place from eight years of a Shenzhen
temporary residence permit.
The assembly line is like rice, words drop into the soup as though
hovering there.
The bottom of the bowl is inscribed with other people's happiness and
misfortune, like snake oil rubbed on the face of our country.
The hardware factory's severed finger drops into the bowl, an overcooked
three-meal life.
The May 12th earthquake followed by a train in Wenzhou, bowls that
make no sound when they break;
five kids from Guizhou and more innocent lives, tossing and turning
under the bowl.
Gutter oil fries up a bit of pity, bad breath infects everything.
A treasured but late-maturing race wants to play doctor to the king.
They start to give themselves medical certificates, start demanding
certificates of health from great men:
Confucious, Mao Zedong, Deng Xiaoping are in quarantine for SARS,
the people see their health has long been failing.

A porcelain country,
with flimsy unfinished walls, so why not heat a few bowls of liquor,
a bowl of cold-resistance, a bowl of courage.

Crowd Sickness

My cavalry
traverses the first blushes of youth.
The hand that cooks
tears the pages from an exercise book,
drags compulsory education into an eight year war,
an underground communist party in my school records.
The emotional seeds of industry
are planted in the sky over the countryside,
growing as quickly as exploded missiles.
A shard shoots into 1998.
From then on there was virtue,
without any backlash.
For every stab of pain there's a factory.
The joints of the workshop
can predict the weather.
The director's husband and the manager's son
are only out for themselves,
and their relatives get dozens of work hours per day.
But I can't be a righteous Judge Bao,
can't break free from my family responsibilities,
can't scream out all the injustices.

Like a Horse at Full Gallop

Back then, I had contempt for the county's hydroelectric station.
Back then, at the Dalang Toy Factory in Dongguan
the throngs of women workers didn't know that I,
a construction worker, would be adding a seventh story onto the six-story
factory.
Back then, the lychee trees to the right were like a huge feral dog,
and the mosquitoes and flies come in swarms
dealing with the construction workers' shit and piss alongside me.

I wanted one kuai, because with a kuai I could get Awen's sister some
instant noodles.
I wanted to tell her, I'm not uneducated, I have a future.
Awen would die before he'd deliver that message.
Back then, construction workers were like foremen's tools, borrowed
and lent.
Awen and I were lent out to Zhushan.
I watched Awen use his own body as a freight elevator.
Then there was a drop, and the elevator's new home became Awen's grave.
My cousin told me, just stay there and keep working, they'll pay you at
New Years and then you'll have some money.

My face fell.
You will never understand what I've suffered.

Alu (b. 1980, Hengnan, Hunan) left to find work in Guangdong when he was eighteen, and at the same time began to write poetry. He has worked as a docker, polisher, warehouse manager, quality control inspector, newspaper editor, and reporter. He now lives in Zhongshan, Guangdong, and works as the head editor for a company magazine.

Purging the Landlords

Today we won't go to work
we're purging the landlords
we've had opening up and reform
but our revolutionary spirit goes on

The landlords have been purged
the land taxes can be shared
if we were given more land
we wouldn't even care

A few quarter-acres of land and a few ridges of wheat
can't compare to a train ticket south
at home the children cry for their mothers
when we're bored we play cards

Those who catch mice are good cats
those who catch kings can be landlords
if my bomb doesn't explode in this restless night
my name isn't Alu

An Elegy for C

I.

These last few years, he hid himself
inside a song. He watched the sun
rise from inside his body

The autumn chill attacked, his
clothing was thin. The noise outside was deafening, he
started dancing alone

These last few years, he liked to go to the square
and sing the same song over and over. He was afraid
if he stopped, a pair of handcuffs would drag him off

Then, he was hit by a falling leaf
it was a fresh, still-steaming leaf
it lay with him on the square, waiting for a sprinkling of rain

2.

As a child he loved
a cloth doll. The quiet nights
were like a pinecone lying in the grass

and many conversations
were like a quick knife: he was afraid
of being sliced open again

The spring was like
a meddlesome matchmaker: he imagined a mountainside
covered in flowers

The city he lived in
was covered with piles of rusted iron
and reflective glass

3.

Twenty years ago
he was a top student. He folded his textbook
into the shape of a train, and hid under his quilt practicing his songs

Ten years ago
he was a construction worker. Each full moon
looked like a chunk of homesick iron

After that, he took a knife
and ran into a crowd. He slashed
a floating northbound cloud

After that, he was chased by a secret government document
after that, he hid inside someone else's dream
even though he himself had never had a dream

4.

He'd once dreamed of this train. An iron-coated suitcase.
He'd once dreamed of sitting in the dark night
fleeing on a southbound train

"It swallowed us, and I liked being
swallowed by it." Hey, do you want a cheap seat or a soft sleeper.
Do you want rice wine or a soft drink. Hey, mister, come buy a flower

Look at this flower with its rosy face, it'll bring love
and good fortune. It'll bring work and money. Look at this flower, it has
a secret for you: keep heading south. Keep drinking. Look at this flower

It symbolizes your lot in life: it doesn't depend on parents or on friends
its work history is more winding than this train
its love life is more elusive than the spring

(This is all just
a made-up hypothesis, like a penciled
self-portrait.)

Occupation: He stands on the pedestrian bridge inspecting
  the many visitors.
Age: He sticks out his hand to block the speeding cars.
Name: The hand he sticks out ends up injuring a foraging ant.

(This is merely a gradual
murder. The knife is disinfected with alcohol. The birds overhead
keep flying north.)

Ideas: He suddenly thinks of fire. The shadows penetrate his thoughts.
Education: The shadows begin to flee. The stars twinkle.
Place of birth: He shuts the window, hides in a suitcase and sobs.

6.

On a piece of paper he writes
his name. Those scrawled names
were sealed up as final evidence

He sees a hand
coming through the wall
to peel a tangerine, to peel off his clothes

An unexpected conversation, encircling an unfolding sale
he brings his song into
an impregnable castle. "In the end, I'm still going to drink

this glass of beer." His name gives him permission.
His name rejects him.
His song brings him back to his faraway home.

7.

He sees a police van
parked at each exit. He folds up his shadow
and sticks it in his suitcase, just in case.

It's dawn now. His body
is like a derailed train
stopped in the rain

He fears the sound of knocking.
He fears the sound of footsteps
climbing the stairs. He unfolds his own shadow

and it becomes someone else. Oh, ID cards. Documents and IDs.
He shakes hands with his shadow. He hands out his name card
to every suspicious person

8.

He falls in love with a girl in a gray uniform
she's like a plastic toy stuck into the night. He prepares
water, a glass bowl, and goldfish

He falls in love with a lotus flower
girl in long braids. And a girl by a window in lipstick.
(Along the way, he falls in love with some rented rooms on the hallway,

some cheap cigarettes in his fingers, and a stranger who bickers endlessly
over a game of cards. He falls in love
with each shadow peddling a bicycle home from work.)

In the end, he falls in love with an apple with a clearly marked price.
He makes himself just like the apple,
sitting on the bed, on guard against the knife on the fruit plate.

9.

"I fell in love with her unfamiliar
chrysanthemum name. I fell in love
with her silhouette in the mirror"—

But the mirror
was like a magic house. And in the mirror
lived a snake with ulterior motives.

"I fell in love with her and her innate
gender. I fell in love with her
dream, more transparent than glass"—

But in the end, no one guessed the snake's
intentions. And in the end,
the mirror defeated our courage

10.

"I believe in spring. I believe in flowers. I believe
in banners flying in the wind." He's like a collector's
gramophone. When he talks about the past, his voice is like a lithe snake—

But the lamplight is like a former lover
rising in someone else's window. In the dark he releases
his youthful groin.

"I believe in roads. I believe in long distance
trains. I believe in freely flying birds.
I believe in overcast skies"—

But in the end, all the flowers resembled
the same flower. When he said I love
they all burst open on the imagined mountainside

11.

Head lowered, he came and then left.
The fog pierced him, like piercing
a shadow

Those things he had known well
the people, places, times
were like sentences written on a piece of paper

ripped up, lost, and then
picked up again, and with a lot of time
patiently pieced back together

After there was a slow feeling of loss
like mending
a coat worn for many years

12.

He watches a bird flying over a haystack
and it doesn't come back. He dreams he is that bird
spreading his wings over the fields

He watches a man walking into the fog
and he doesn't come back. He dreams he is that man
dragging his tired body further and further away

Ah, these wonderful
transient shadows
piled there like a childhood snowdrift

But his body troubles him—
this naked body
that slowly huddles up in the dark

13.

Like a flock of birds
flying over this withered forest

But the corners of his mouth lift slightly
the moment is peaceful

The grasses outside, the wind carrying fine rain
and these useless old instruments

He is as he usually is
hiding in a corner smoking

or he's like a child, curiously
sizing himself up

Zheng Xiaoqiong (b. 1980, Nanchong, Sichuan) worked for six months in a rural hospital after graduating from nursing school, and then moved to Dongguan to work in a die-mold factory. She worked in a toy factory, a magnetic tape factory, and as a hole-punch operator in a hardware factory for five years. She is now an editor at a magazine. Her poetry collections include *Huangma Mountains, Collected Poems of Zheng Xiaoqiong, Pedestrian Bridge,* and *Poems Falling on Machines.*

Life

What you don't know is that my name has been hidden by an employee ID
my two hands have become part of the assembly line, my body was signed over
to a contract, my black hair is turning white, leaving noise and toil
overtime work and wages...I've passed through fixed fluorescent lights
and the exhausted shadows flung on the machine stations move slowly
turning, bending down, silent as cast iron
oh, iron that speaks in sign language, covered with the disappointment and
grief of migrants
iron that rusts over time, iron that trembles in the midst of reality—
I don't know how to protect a silent life
this life of a lost name and gender, this life of surviving off of contracts
where and how do I start, with the moon on the metal cots in the eight-
person dorm room
what it illuminates is homesickness, the secret flirting and love in the
thundering of the machines,
or youth stopped by a timesheet, and how in the middle of this restless life
can one console a frail soul, if the moonlight comes from Sichuan
then my childhood is lit by memories, extinguished by a seven-day assembly
line workweek
what's left, these blueprints, iron, metal products, or white
inspection labels, red defective goods, and under the fluorescent lights, the
loneliness and pain
I bear, in all this toil, is hot and endless......

Iron

Small iron, soft iron, blown by the wind
pounded by the rain, iron reveals its rusty cowardice and timidity
the conclusion of last year…was like time dripping through a pinhole
how much iron is there in the night, in the open warehouse, on the work
stations…where
does it want to go, and where will it be taken? How much iron
questions itself at night, how much is
rusting with a rustle, while at night who
claims life's past and future in the midst of their ironlike lives

What else doesn't rust? Last year followed a container car
to someplace far away, this year is still flowing between the fingers
next year is a piece of iron about to arrive, awaiting the blueprints
machine stations, order forms, but at this moment, where am I and where
will I go
"Life is like a stove fire burning, roiling."
My outsider's timidity is rusting in my body
I alone, or a group of people

and a handful of iron, iron that has kept silent for years
iron that can leave at any time, iron that can return at any time,
rusting in the rustling flow of time, staring into the distance
yearning to take root like the iron-grated window beside me

Industrial Zone

The fluorescent lights are lit, the buildings are lit, the machines are lit
exhaustion is lit, the blueprints are lit....
this is Sunday night, this is the night of August 15th
the moon lights up a disk of emptiness, in the lychee trees
a light breeze sways an internal whiteness, many years of speechless
quiet, in the evergreen grasses the insects hum, the city's lights illuminate
the industrial zone, so many dialects, so much homesickness,
so many weak and insubstantial bodies placed there, so much moonlight
shining
on Sunday's machines and blueprints, and it rises
to shine on my face, a slowly dropping heart

So many lamps are lit, so many people pass by
the lamps, the past, and the workstations of the industrial zone
that mute moonlight, lamplight and me
so much paltriness, small as spare parts, filaments
using their feeble bodies to warm the industrial zone's bustle and noise

And the tears, joy, and pain we've had
our glorious or petty ideas, and our souls
are all illuminated by the moonlight, collected, and carried afar
hidden in rays of light no one will notice

They

I remember iron, iron that rusted over time
pale red or dark brown, tears in a furnace fire
I remember the distracted, exhausted eyes above the workstations
their gazes were small and trivial, small as a gradual furnace fire
their depression and distress, and a tiny bit of hope
are lit up by the flames, unfold, on white blueprints
or between the red lines of a traditional painting, by the meager monthly
        wages
and a gradually exhausted heart—

I remember their faces, their wild eyes and subtle trembling
their calloused fingers, their rough and simple lives
I say quietly: they are me, I am them
our grief and pain and hope are kept silent and forbearing
our confessions and hearts and loves are all in tears,
all is as silent and lonely as iron, or as pain

I say, in the vast crowds, we are all alike
we all love and hate, we all breathe, we all have noble spirits
we all have unyielding loneliness and compassion!

Time

In the village where I've lived for six years, in the lychee grove
the mountain stream shines on my truncated youth
the hardware factory's drowsy dream
leaves Silver Lake Park, heading north
I polish a migrant's sighs
and my own closer Huangma Mountain dialect
in the shade of banyan trees, the blazing industrial zone
turns brighter and brighter in the minds of the workers
past events fall from memory, wet
with grief, and the lights show the wrinkles slowly forming at my eyes
a lonely bird hides itself in the darkness of the lychee grove
the darkness overwhelms the red of the lychees, and the dark branches
turn even darker, the birdcalls have faded, and here
the roar of the hardware factory continues its banging unabated
my worker's number is 231, and when I take the blueprints, there in the darkness
in the midst of forgotten time, I see my youth
wriggling away in a clean and public grief
withering in the vastness of my country

A Product's Story

First, it starts with a warped piece of iron sheeting, setting off from a
village, iron mine, truck,
steamer, or port, then losing one's name, getting a serial number, and
standing at a workstation;
second is springs and assembly lines, the whinny of nervous motion, pain
close by, aluminum alloys,
blueprints, breadcrumbs, cutting machines, familiar sweat, plastic and
cardboard boxes,
pleasures and sorrows; third is the pale faces under fluorescent lights,
employee IDs, mechanical springs,
gears, card edge connectors, pressure coolants, anti-rust oil, silent
overtime;
fourth is certificates, standardized forms, exterior polishing, the lashings
of a 3000-degree furnace
the cooling heat treatment of overtime pay, of the raindrops, of being
fired, your twisted-up
body appearing in an hourglass; fifth is temporary residence permits,
physical exam cards, proof of single status,
migrant worker cards, work permits...they wait in line, silently, leaning on
plastic travel bags with exhausted faces; sixth is young pinned-down arms,
back pay
and fines, missed periods, a medical history of flus, listlessness,
homesickness
as wide as the sea, noise from the overhead lights, drifting in a far city and
paystubs floating on a river;
seventh is the dialects of machines and dorms, Hunanese dreams on the
bunk above Sichuanese,
Hubeinese is neighbors with Anhuinese, the Gansunese machine bit off half
of the Jiangxinese's finger, Guangxinese's nightshift, Guizhounese's
gloominess, Yunanese's rainsoaked
sleep-talk and Henanese's dress. Eighth is sticks of fried dough, lumps
of instant noodles, the shape of the city in vegetable soup, masks made of
copper, coupling links, certificates of conformity,
a buck and half of fried rice noodles, chili sauce, artificially flavored and

colored cola;
ninth is love hidden in stories and fairy tales, shared rented rooms, doors
without keys, iron ladders to upper berths, antiseptic fluids in hospitals,
birth control pills, the tears of breaking up,
corroded flesh, baseless promises of love; tenth is train tickets to go home,
a door
or a pit, a quick-selling ticket or a possible fake, squeezed in the aisles,
in the toilet, standing on tiptoe, crushed, you just want to find a place on
the train or in the world
to live, to love, to slowly grow old

Assembly Line

Along with the flow of the assembly line is the flow of people
they come from Hedong or Hexi, she stands or sits, with a number, blue
uniform,
white worker's hat, her fingers on her workstation, her name is A234,
A967, Q36...
either running the controls, loading the shoots, turning screws...

Crossing between the flow of migrant workers and the flow of products,
the women are fish, working night and day, dragging along
the boss's order forms, profit, the GDP, youth, vision, dreams
dragging along the glory of the Industrial Age

In the sounds of the line's flow, they live lonelier lives,
women and men drift past each other as strangers
the women's lives get pushed back in the water, leaving screws in their
hands, pieces of plastic
iron nails, glue, coughing lungs, bodies wracked with occupational diseases,
floating in the flow of temporary work

The assembly line is constantly tightening the valves of the city and destiny,
those yellow
switches, red wires, gray products, the fifth cardboard box
holds plastic lamps, fake Christmas trees, youth trapped on employee IDs,
Li Bai's
burning love turned cold, or still reading his poetry softly: oh, so romantic!

In its understated flow, I see fate flowing
here in a southern city, I lower my head to write quatrains and ballads of
this Industrial Age

Witnessed

Noises
of gears
iron sheets
synthesizers
plastics
they roll, scrape, scream, shout

drowsiness grows on her skin at four a.m.

noises
of cutting
polishing
drilling
striking
they flow, walk, run, pause

drowsiness grows in her body at four a.m.

noises
of curses
hearts
yawns
exhaustion
they mix, tangle, twist, pile up

drowsiness grows in her bones at four a.m.

at four a.m. I witnessed her drowsiness grow wooden
I witnessed her finger let the machine take a bite
I witnessed the spray of blood wake her from drowsiness
I witnessed her crying, her screams
I witnessed our sighs, our helplessness

and then, the noises started up again
and then, the drowsiness started to grow again

and then…
came silence

Language

I speak this sharp-edged, oiled language
of cast iron—the language of silent workers
a language of tightened screws   the crimping and memories of iron sheets
a language like callouses   fierce   crying   unlucky
hurting   hungry language   back pay of the machines' roar   occupational
        diseases
language of severed fingers   life's foundational language   in the dark
        place of unemployment
between the damp steel bars   these sad languages

..........I speak them softly

in the roar of the machines. A dark language. Language of sweat. Rusty
        language
like a young woman worker's helpless eyes or an injured male worker by
        the factory doors
their hurting language   language of shivering bodies
language of denied compensation for injured fingers

Rust-speckled switches, stations, laws, the system. I speak a black-blooded
        fired language
of status, age, disease, finances...a fearful, howling language. Tax collectors
        and petty officials.
Factory bosses. Temporary residence permits. Migrant workers...their
        languages
language of a girl jumping off a building. The GDP's language. Language
        of official projects. Language of a kid's school fees.

I speak of stone. Of overtime. Violent language
I speak of...the abyss. Climbing the ladder. Unreachable distances
the language of holding life's railings in the gusts of fruitless labor

I speak—

these sharp-edged oiled languages, their pointy edges open up
to stab this soft era!

Workshop Love

My fantasies away toil in the dark workshop.....
the cast iron machine console ponderously droops its horsehead top
behind the burnished steel strip   behind the temporary darkness
            and silence
your oily fingers and piercing eyes   your chest
is steady as a hydraulic press—full of scorching roiling passion
gentleness flows from my thick bent fingers.....
amber lips   iron   blueprints   bright metal indictors
my tongue   love   torsos   switches   the force of a turning screwdriver
fate and memory   you in the darkness   sourness of sweat
oil streaks on arms   those strands of messy black hair
blue breakfast smoke caught in the stomach   the cramped workshop
I feel the tenderness between callouses   with its rose-red
love......in the awkward handwriting of the workshop's certificates
what's written in blue ballpoint pen is longing   what's written in red
is love   and the white paper shows your oily fingerprints
and your body's warmth   black film   bent shoots
the horsehead machine like your shadow   moves slowly
life's machine creaks and squeaks   love flowing from machines
products on the shelves   that violently birthed exhaustion and callouses
thick fingers float over a rough life   but love
the only sign of spring in the workshop   grows.....

Woman Worker: Youth Pinned to a Station

Time opens its enormous maw   the moon on the machine
rusting   tired   darkened   turbid   its inner danger
gurgles past   the cliff of the body collapses   into mud and splintered
stones
the splinters of time   turbulent waters fill a woman's body
wild tidal waters no longer fluctuating with the seasons   she sits at her
station
the flowing products and interlocking time   are swallowed up   quickly
aging   ten years flowing past like water   enormous weariness
floats through the mind   for many years   she's stuck by the side
of the screws   one screw   two screws   turning   to the left   to the right
fixing her dreams and her youth to some product   look
at her pale youth   running   from an inland village
to a factory by the sea   all the way to a shelf in America
fatigue and occupational diseases build up in the lungs
get caught in the throat   a lifetime of irregular periods
fierce coughing   the distant development zone full of factories
the green lychee trees cut down   the machines by her side
shivering   she rubs her swollen red eyes   and sticks herself back
into the flow of products

Moonlight: Married Workers Living Apart

Moonlight washes the steel faces, the moonlight leaves a line of footprints
on the iron vines of the security wall
the moonlight lengthens the distance between buildings 5 and 6, from the
female dorm
to the male dorm, the moonlight stops in the window for a minute, the moon
illuminates him, or her
the moonlight illuminates their bodies, skeletons, inner desires, the moon
light illuminates
their memories of their wedding night, the moonlight is too bright
like salt poured into the wound of living apart eighteen days after their
marriage

Moonlight illuminates the well in their bodies, illuminates the well of desire
the moonlight illuminates their fifteen-day honeymoon, illuminates his
memory
of her body taken over by shade inch by inch, privet fruit trees
her body lies fallow in the moonlight, inch by inch
slipping along the 45 meters between buildings 5 and 6

If the moonlight were a bit closer, the far expanse it brings in would be
bigger
her desire would be a bit deeper, if the moonlight were a bit darker
the wounds on her skin would be a bit wider, his inner torture would be
a bit deeper

Moonlight illuminates the unfinished building for married workers, the
moonlight shines on an article in the paper
"The Sex Lives of Migrant Workers….."
if the moonlight were a bit darker, love would be a bit stronger
if the moonlight were a bit brighter, the planned rooms for married
couples would be a bit larger

Kneeling Workers Demanding Their Pay

The women flash by like ghosts   at bus stops
machine stations   industrial zones   filthy rented rooms
their thin bodies   are like razor blades   like white paper
like strands of hair   like the air   they use their fingers to slice
iron   film   plastics   their exhausted numb
faces are like ghosts   they're stuffed into machine stations
work uniforms   assembly lines   their bright gazes
young ages   they hide in their self-constructed
dark tidal currents   I can't tell them apart anymore
just like no one can tell me apart from them   leftover leathery
bodies   motion   blurred faces   one after another
innocent faces   they're constantly put together   arranged
into an electronics factory ants nest   a toy factory honeycomb   they
laugh   stand   kneel   bend   huddle
they've been simplified down to fingers   and legs
they've become tightened screws   sliced iron sheets
compressed plastic   bent aluminum wire   cut cloth
their expressions of disappointment   pride   exhaustion   happiness
chaos   helplessness   loneliness
they come from villages   hamlets   valleys   neighborhoods   they're smart
clumsy   timid   weak
today they kneel   facing the big bright window
the black-uniformed guards   the shiny cars   the green bushes
the dazzling factory sign glints in the sun
they kneel at the factory entrance   holding a cardboard sign
with the scrawled words   Give us our hard-earned money
the four women kneel in the factory entrance without fear
a group of onlookers has surrounded them   for several days   people
from the same village
coworkers   friends   or those who work the same workstations
they watch the kneeling women impassively
they witness their four coworkers dragged off by the guards   they
witness
one of the worker's shoes falling off   they witness another worker's

pants ripped in the struggle   they watch silently
as the four workers are dragged somewhere far away   their eyes
hold no sorrow   and no pleasure   they impassively enter the factory
it depresses me no end

In the Hardware Factory

God's as lazy as we are and produced humans on an assembly line
I could find my other half anywhere
they're as standardized as goods made in a factory,
a marriage gives rise to thorns of resentment, from noon to sunset
you live among the thorns, the pain is hard to bear, thinking of the pretty
  girl in the mirror
thinking of bone diseases, thinking of the conventions of Chinese medicine
you hear death's name, and it's like a piece of steel
inlayed in your bones, you can't afford to be sick,
a butterfly flapping is wings inside a 3000-degree boiler
you'll think it was a beast in a past life
running across an African savanna, but your disease started with the beast
of the machine, from levers to screws, from blueprints to calipers
from loneliness to a lost youth, it smells of hardware factory tools
and you're nothing but a lump of iron, thinking of words that have to do
  with iron
like sheen, iron oxide, cast iron, steel, thinking of its sharpness
and the pain it causes as it pricks the body, thinking of its enormous
spindles, pulverizing a dream into powder, thinking of its steel needle
sewing up a wound, and if you need
to emerge from love in the midst of labor laws, smearing bread with butter
in the midst of hope, these nighttime machines at 11:14pm
these thoughts wriggle like fish as she huddles between the calipers
and there is a different world outside, with its songs of debauchery

A lion would have trouble reaching the tip of a thought of steel
a steel monster has her by the throat, and in its bones
are violent rain and thunder, heartfelt fantasies, and the iron turns from
  black to red
turns cold and dusty like frost in my stomach
or it installs itself in the gears or levers or pulleys of the era
we need an energy-saving era, but all the inferior goods
are turned into a symbol of iron by my abandoned organs, it was once
a nostalgic spring equinox, stove fires lit the many metaphors and symbols

you made genitals out of steel, made them hard
the basis of Chinese medicine is the moon, waxing and waning
you cut patterns of a cross, a sun, a penis at your cutting machine
and the thunder brings silver wings across the sky, steel has its own
mouth and taste, it must use sliding calipers or a compass to calibrate
the hunger of this era, the officials are anxious to learn, the poor are used
        to crying
the countryside has learned to be polluted, the city is being demolished
torn down, demolished, torn down
our diminishing bodies feel the unformed future
and his designs depart from realism, the Romantics
start to feed on illusion, our futures get better and better, just keep on
signing real contracts with blind men, he imagines plums on the southern
        mountains
and he tells us that the eggs in his hands are rocks
time seems set apart from the Four Modernizations of the '80s
I still haven't made it to the 21st century's low slope of prosperity
the mountains are so high, but the body rots, and how many years will it take
to reach utopia, I pity myself as I age
unable to squeeze onto communism's last train
but living in a scorching workshop in a sweatshop
like an autumn cicada ready to cast off its shell, unnamable, unsummonable,
        impassable,
trustworthy time, ideal sunlight, an obscure silent future
beside the new century is a pile of machine-cut trash and social stages
that came too late to complete, time begins to defect
it laughs at our memories and enthusiasm as they slip away, and you don't
        stop your praises
nothing can absorb more than empty time
I long for the past, twenty years of a turned loom spins a classic thread
the needle of the Great Leap Forward sewed the clothes of reform and
        opening up,
the bureaucrats' livers turn black, but they're black enough already
so much has been destroyed, what's left is an unbroken eulogy
oh, these goddamn soft bones, he always planned to use
wings of lies to step on the moon, the poor man, so servile
I'm accustomed to breaking iron, polishing it, drilling holes, creating the

exterior
of this era, arranging my fate on top of pieces of ironware
a grand banquet requires worry as alcohol, poverty as food
what does this world have to offer me aside from grief, what else
can console us, living these difficult lives.....

The reality is princes and party bosses, tax collectors and organizations,
on rainy days
they hold meetings to discuss the country's yin and yang, the roads, ideology,
how there's a need
for more email attachments and ordinances, how trees need steel altars, the
moon will be reborn
in water, these guesses should be rewarded, its bewitching passwords come
from Grave-Sweeping Day
the powers of the elders, its cheekbones are too high, her fate is too terrible,
her poetry
is too good, leaving goals that are too hard, stabbing into this soft era
in her last life she was a phoenix, reborn as a lion, and the steel is too black
the isms too many, leaving her shapely body to surrender to the world,
together with the night
appearing, intersecting, coinciding, and they have identical faces
it already can't return to the prairie, its definition is expanding, extending
the leftover seeds from Grain Rain Day to bring you good luck
morality is fragile, its body is skewered on steel shamelessness, the spiders
spin webs
the moths leap to flame, I can't avoid the building's lean, its arrogant
expression
and the remaining warmth of Naturalism's adherents, they feel fine but
have lost confidence
still sunk in the self-pitying elegant scenery of the past, she comes from
the Sichuan countryside
the hometown of milkvetch, returning from forests to steel, bleak heart
filled with ivy
polishing poetry between machines, molding it with iron and blueprints,
so life is
this toil, the burning heat of the hardware factory workshop, electric saws
and steel hammers, the sago palms on the windowsill, the palms outside

and traditional woods, they're formed into frames, strips, shapes, like
ancient doctrines
you hold tight to Japanese silk roses, German gears, imitation calipers, it's
tragic, this imitation factory
starts to produce counterfeit boxes and lids, they're like coffin after coffin,
filled with my soul
they're independent from your body and heart, they hold endless secrets
the draftsmen sink into lines, the molders craft by appearance,
statisticians compute numbers, bosses calculate profits, while I do overtime
overnight
and the moon in the window only lights up my dreams, the quality inspector
stamps in red
signs her name and adds her number, I face the cold steel and the
unresponsive vastness
memory lies in waste like the development zones, gazing at ancient temples
surrounded by factories
there are some deserted old ways that seem like ruins or relics, *the air
shakes the scent of hemp*
I write this line on the back of graph paper, and the shaking will be passed
from the paper to the flesh, if I still need to explain, I get used to abstractions
and comfortable seats along with the production supervisor
she has a tongue like fine iron wire, twisting around order forms and
customers, the overhead lights
illuminate my doctrines and notations, and the iron pincers and knives
head my way, she flips the switch
and turns on disease, and the iron on the machine is polished, rounded,
squared, corrugated, left
or right, oh, I'm a loyal worker, the gears catch as they turn, and the iron
bars turn
into toys, VCDs, the silent iron will be given a rare long journey
the thread-cutter thrusts out a crablike pincer, grabbing onto Confucius's
poetry, thoughts, and profits,
grains of life's original quiet, lifting toward the shady places like the
production supervisor's skirt, and all night the lamp
lights up a blueprint for the future, oh, these threads are fairly simple,
these doctrines have some mistakes
I open the valve to life, this postmodern art, what do springtime's dark

ghosts need
the iron is forged, its wet silhouette blooms in the iron webbing, it wears
a black iron coat, carries a black iron scarf, oh, you lift your head to look
at the clock at the top of the church
now, my blood pressure skyrockets, it rises with our collective shame
for so many years, I haven't kept up with the isms, politics' swimming
champions grow
scales, the bell's ring lives on in time, and time is so long and life is so short
what's left of the city lacks education, it tries to start a red-light district,
big hotels
raise bright mosaics, it's just a shame that the old houses that have held
out don't understand a harmonious society
these defective kids and products, the strange odor filling my life
will they come into bloom, will they wither and fall, look at the workshop's
polisher
who starts to stick out a defecting finger, life was once a trade and her
back is to the rock,
a lonely heart, overtime in a sweating factory has destroyed my heart, I'm
like a prisoner
who has given up freedom for a rebirth, oh, there are still three work steps
left, rivet joints
soldering, and isn't it like a beast biting into you, iron shavings flying,
with so many nightmares, we need someone to warm our sleep

As soon as I could I left this life of iron, it carried out a kind of
Romanticism
on the machines, pulled dreams from the last punched hole, left behind a
hundred shapes
and a hundred futures, as I bear loneliness in the shrieks of iron, it carved
my residence registration on a hole-punch, my age, records, temporary
residence permits, it records it all
my work number and jobs, it forges a jail cell, and uses production
numbers to track
our emotional states, its blueprints are dusky theories, requiring
philosophy and political theory
iron is delivering a speech on the machines, it's waiting for the name of a
theory or a style

I'm already used to a fantastical realism, worshipping the mute, now it's
perfect for
a kind of opening up, from ore to iron, from iron to products, this is
the process of iron establishing a political party, it uses calipers, blueprints,
switches, yes
and there's electricity, those words you softly muttered, like water
flowing through your nerves, you tremble and read out electricity, iron
turns electricity
into party regulations and power, these collective parties of iron tools
start to tell me what to do
drill holes here, fold there, it speaks in translation, good at guarding against
the mixed grief and confusion of the ordinary people, it matches my inner
thoughts
the molding designer starts drafting economic policy and advancing the
system of roads
finding the main points on an iron plate, the center of iron, organizing
principles,
the thread-cutter is busy with plans and development, planning a
development zone on an iron plate
the central zone, where they forge a subpar financial center, the sharp
whistles of the machines
are the last home-owning holdouts having their houses torn down,
relocated, the toiling hardware factory's polisher,
hole-puncher, and cutter, who live with their relatives in one room, use a
ruthless measure
to mold iron lives, they are confined there to polish, punch, and bore
the size and depth must be harmonious and stable, the textbooks repeat
the political ideology
they must learn forbearance, this is a separate China of unemployment,
layoffs,
job injuries, severed fingers, oh, these simple people prevented from living
in the city
the representatives give speeches, the Central Consultative Conference puts
forward proposals, while elementary students explain in their homework
to create a clean and tourist-friendly city, migrant workers must be
forbidden from crowding in
they live in the shame of an iron-sheet country, so many of their hearts are

weak
they can't take X pounds of pain, they get stomach problems and
occupational diseases
and kidney stones, their blood vessels are stuffed with dissatisfaction and
grudges, made sick for the iron country
bringing elements of destabilization, and petitioners begin to enter the
next sequence
product inspectors begin to pick undesirables, familiar iron bars show another
face
the scarred winning competitors are too humorous and righteous, they
will not yield
to a single doctrine, and we begin to use computer bits and forms to
express happiness
time is like a pork pie, it lacks a birthplace and an identity, it is filled with
too much dissent
we must wait for the custodians to come and clean, this iron will exchange
its tongue and mouth
its personality makes it excellent in a chorus, it uses satire and rhetorical
tricks
to recite the comedies of life, while the foreign factory's quality control
points in only one direction
she starts to point at the nation of iron, her voice is filled
with calls for the dead and for alchemy, this iron needs work with a
stronger political bent
with the poems and art of existence, iron is too quiet
it hasn't cast off the old customs, it won't face the customer gods
and flirt, we need revisions and deletions, for time to return
to 1990, our transformations need to be examined anew
these restless years need to be debated and corrected
of mistakes, iron's matrix is stuck in the 1980s
its dull stiff circles don't work in the new age, the molding designers need
to be woken, they've stood too long in the advantages of the past
or they're too close to the bureaucrats of old and the new VIPs
their designs aren't right for the masses, the thread-cutter cares too much
about profits, leaving out the curved lines of ordinary people, leaving
behind the polishers,
hole-punchers, cutters, who are made responsible for inferior goods, and

the suffering
iron's hesitant despair makes dead politicians take responsibility, and just as we
have never felt grief for no reason, the dead can pardon them
to arrive at memories and symbols even emptier than iron's political party, the bosses
must pay respects to useless objects, the statisticians calculate mistakes and defects
her handwriting is terrible, it makes my pay seem confusing
sickening my heart, and under the stares of collectivism we learn
how distrust and habit and lack of habit replace force, I think rebellion
cannot but play the role of loyal workers, punching the time clock right on time, respectful of superiors
brains are washed by iron's political party, there are eyes everywhere
it glistens in a crab-claw light, getting a vice-grip on excess ideas and imagination
the security guards are good at violence, guarding the doors and searching bodies, their blue uniforms
are as forbidding as policemen's, they inspect the workshops, hand out fines to those they find napping

Now I return to the center of iron, and where is it from
a mountain's depths, a coalmine, a foreign country, it was once a buried stone
dug up by someone, pulverized, it holds the earth's coughing
its dark gray body is wracked by late-stage disease, iron's past
is so desolate I don't dare imagine any more, it's passed through tall buildings, factories,
railways and state-run processing plants, they're installed even deeper in the machines than the earth
its hopes need the hacksaw and spark machine, I use a mute language to speak
of their desires, returning to the mood of rocks, it can't speak Chinese
the hardest place of the Han, I can only indistinctly hear it, it sounds like rocks
crying, it comes from a handmade cellar, and the way back has been sealed up by industry and the city guards

it's traveling a corridor made of nonfiction, from stone to iron
from iron to product, it encounters nonstop time
they are cut into incomplete shapes, yesterday, today, tomorrow,
history, the future, the present, or the 21st century, it's all fragments of you
or me, you want to insist on the old doctrines, tossed by life, pushed aside
life cannot tolerate overly perfect things, it has a dangerous
jealous heart, it starts to end, and I'm still longing for ancient times as I
    stand at this modern machine
longing to go back to the Tang—to write poetry, collect Chinese medicine
    on the mountainsides, go fishing in the wind and fine rain

Cheng Peng (b. 1980, Kaxian, Chongqing) finished middle school and then began to work as a construction worker, repairman, and assembly line worker. He started writing poetry in 2005.

Abandoned Village

Peaceful Village is in a gully, where the day is a lid
covering a hundred li, the mountain is cold water and a ladle, the village
water-level keeps dropping. There are less than a thousand people.
Now only children and the elderly are left. The old men plow for three
months, the old women weakly hoe the grain
children chase chickens to the coops, the setting sun slants
over the slope's stalks and grasses, the fields birth brambles and branches,
the tangerines and pomelos grow old
mothers leave a month after giving birth, and grandmothers take over
at eighteen they leave looking for work, forty sons and daughters off in
search of jobs
they rarely come back, their kids don't know them,
they call them auntie, then big sister
the school has closed down, the teacher gone to the city to look for work.
Villages merge
and a woman takes over, an old man replaces the village's female
representative
his oldest daughter leaves to find work and marries someone from a far
province, their closeness broken
his oldest son leaves to find work, goes to the city, starts scalping drugs,
gets sent to jail
his second son works construction, moving bricks and sweating buckets,
he demands his pay and goes to prison on a knife's edge
his third son severs his left hand with a cutting machine and has no
livelihood. The old man scans
the village from one end to the other, the river polluted from industry.

From one end of the village to the other, people play cards and gamble
the fat uncles learn from the city how to keep mistresses
they haven't seen the old man for years, and there are more graves
the green hills have no smoke, a swath of blue-green, growing more distant

Homesick

I live on a screw's sharp word-awn
I stand on the hard-up painful center of a sentence-edge
I'm hopelessly squeezed in the pliers' poem-howl

From beginning to middle to end
the homesick sunset is stuck in rhymes of fatigue and shame
my thoughts roam toward the future

Song of Construction Workers

We built it! The flower-gardened villas. Where you live
you so-called princelings, owners of the city
we're the same age, you walk dogs, dogs of noble blood
but they're still mutts. That glare at what we're doing

Our construction worker blood is inlaid with the bricks
to shelter you from wind and rain. You so-called high officials and VIPs
magnates, national cadres, public servants. I want to wake you with my
  screams
use your conscience to measure the weight of our aluminum souls

National sites, official buildings, government halls, mayoral mansions
we built them! We built those thresholds for you, ones we can no longer
  cross
we built the Labor Law Building, where someone is dozing
we built the People's Mansion, which we can only gaze at

Picks and hammers rust into our rallying banner
let my poetry to call to you!
On the great road to communism, so many ghosts
can't return home. We built it!

Chi Moshu (b. 1980, Yifeng, Jiangxi) grew up with a coal miner father who lost his job. After graduating from high school in 1999, he worked in Dongguan on assembly lines, and as a porter, print shop worker, rubber worker, deliveryman, and warehouse manager. His poetry collections include *Coal Miner Father* and *Branching Dazzling Sunshine*. He has also written books of essays and poetry for children.

In the Factory

I hear the exhaust fan whumping
light and shadow appear in my dark corner

A pattern, a flash, "the world is a swindler"
I sit in a corner of the workshop
totally drained, stomach in pain
and clothing soaked in paint
my fingers smelling of methylbenzene

A mix of colors appears under my printing die
off-colors, raw edges, air holes, dislocations, low luminosity
it's no good

The manager flings the defective piece
at my and my coworkers' feet with a crash

I lower my head, as the curses thunder
my head is abuzz

Whose slap is this, like a shimmering knife
light and shadow appear in my dark corner

The South's Dilemma

Too much talk, the words get worn out.
These poor, sweet adjectives
are sacrificed to modern industry.

Other sentences are stuck on the assembly line.
In Dongguan, the whole Pearl River Delta
turns into a dilapidated wall:
blazing lights glimpsed through a gap.

A fabrication or replacement?
The stars are all asleep
and the 24-hour machines are still there
like sleeping babies shaken awake.

At the end of each day, lies whinny through the night.
Sunday is just an extra shift. Sweat and blood
are hidden in the impoverished alleys and sewers;
all the glory gets engraved into memorial stones, sprayed
into the language of advertising.

From order forms, managers, purchasing, production,
and warehouses, then to container cars with heads held high
rushing down the highway to the wharfs

Can it be that we and our lives
are mere flesh-accessories to the machines?

Oh, how many more soundless cries will there be
and how many more people will lose their hometowns

And each morning before the shift we shout:
Good! Great! Fantastic!

Lord, living in this moment
is so beautiful it seems real!

The Baths at the Hardware Factory

I've been in many hardware factories, and seen many kinds of baths
cooling-off baths, rust-removing baths, electroplating baths
in the baths, the iron
shrieks, but you and I
can't hear it

What I've seen most of
is rust-removing baths
where processed and unprocessed
iron needing rust removed
is picked up by movable pulley
and sunk deep into the bath

A lot of sulfuric acid is added to the bath
along with rust-remover and other chemicals
in its depths the iron struggles
I've watched
it fizz and bubble up

The operator wears
acid/alkali corrosion protective
clothing, gloves, rubber boots
his whole body bundled up
at one moment's distraction, his skin
will be a huge hole

This is a kind of purgatory
a torture for metal
a torment of death and rebirth
of several hours, or longer
to make it new, the iron is put into a water bath
and then is thrust into the forge

That bath of sulfuric acid
is wastewater
and when the sluice opens, the chemical sewage
drains straight down to the sewers—

In the Rubber Factory

Rubber Factory Processes

A Banbury mixer, raw material, cooling off
crushing, sheeting, cooling off
cutting, die-casting, finishing

Banbury Mixer

The Banbury mixer, an enormous internal batch mixer
towers from the first floor up to the second
the Banbury has an enormous engine
and an enormous stomach
turning 24 hours a day
digesting highly elastic rubber

Open its mouth
and throw in all kinds of gum, raw petroleum, and white carbon
press the button, revolve and revolve
for 20 minutes, or 30 minutes
the temperature rising to 100° C, or higher
let it all roast inside its belly
let all of the chemicals
mix evenly into rubber

The hardness of white carbon
the softness of petroleum
how much you add affects the hardness of the rubber
if you want it to be resistant to wear
add so many grams
according to the formula
you have to watch the machine panel constantly
the time and temperature dials
one mistake

and it all has to be redone
they'll fine you, and the offense will be recorded

Plastics Crusher

The plastics crusher takes unfinished rubber
and processes it with the primary chemical:
sulfur
also white carbon and colored gum
to turn it white, black, yellow, red....
as soon as it's been processed, its properties are set
if it isn't worked within 24 hours, it turns to waste
like the old rubber soles
that lie unchanging in garbage dumps for a hundred years

Two enormous plastic crushers turn their pressurized steel drums
sulfur burns within them, spurting out chemicals
like fireworks. When my coworkers
get off work their hair has hardened to steel wire

In the Rubber Factory

At the safety meeting, a factory cadre
told us a story
he said, you have to be quick on the plastic crusher's brakes
there used to be only a handbrake and no footbrake
a while ago there was a guy
who was reversing the spin and got his glove caught in the rolling steel drum
and the glove got rubber on it
and his hand got drawn into the rubber
his other hand tried to find the handbrake but couldn't reach it
and so, turn by turn
his palm began to be crushed, but he didn't feel the pain
and didn't call for help. Then half his arm had been pulled in
and then his entire body was inside the rolling rubber

when people realized what had happened
the steel drum was still turning, and a head was rolling on the surface
(at that point, the cadre laughed and spoke louder)
in the machine's chassis they found blood and crushed flesh
but they never found out what happened to the bones

Die-Casting

Pull out the die
open it and pull out a shoe sole mold
fill it with raw material
stick it back in the die
and that's die-casting

The hydraulic press will automatically start
heating up quickly
it can get up to 300 degrees

The dies are heavy
if one falls
and connects with a foot
the bone will shatter

The temperature is so high
that throughout the day
one worker
can down two and a half gallons of water

In the Print Shop

Odors

The odors drift between fingers, a plant's sorrow
hovering in the air. I'm afraid to speak
the women's names, their youthful faces
the stinging wounds in their smooth skin and ache
in their stomachs, they're already used to breathing
corroded air in the dark. These numb hearts
speak of sulfur, glue, methylbenzene, speak of shampoo
bodywash, perfume, speak of love in the moonlight
these sweet things are like dewdrops at dawn
like the East River's incessant sobbing waters

Stomach

This vast landscape is like a stomach
the small station where the train stops for three minutes
the midnight hunger, fifteen woven-plastic bags
crammed in together. Squirming in the compartment, contorted
and damaged. We need a broad expanse
but the stomach contracts, spitting up disobedient bile
the dark hiding the distance, painful worrying
like a mobile workshop, ah, printing
ink and methylbenzene flow from my palms
veins like gutters, my bones are like iron strips under the press
they are numb with a loss of hope
and my stomach turns picky, greens, turnips, tofu
water spinach, potatoes, no oil to cook in and no meat
but now, facing the chemical lubricants
my appetite expands, squirming
and shouting as though with the pain of burning up

Printing Workshop

The printing workshop is on the fourth floor of the factory
the elevation makes for better venting
and better that the touring visitors on the first floor
not smell the odor of solvents
the printing workshop has a tile floor
and a person assigned to clean up the oily residues
it's the most beautiful workshop in the factory
entering from the elevator or stairs
first is the high frequency welding machine, the injection storage, the ink
storage
and only then does one approach the screen printer
a screen printer is hand-operated
using silkscreens and scrapers as tools
and rubber and PVC as the main materials
as well as sometimes cloth, and in the workshop
they wear street shoes, it's the most esteemed workshop
with high profits and frequent visitors

I once thought of printing
as an elegant patterning, born of my hands
flashing across an athletic field, even an Olympic field
imagine the beauty of the movement
up until my clothing was soaked with ink and solvents
until my skin and my lungs.....
until one of my coworkers
an old employee, was diagnosed with an occupational disease

In the Mirror

He said his hand had become deformed
from the force needed for printing
he said every three days the skin on his fingers flaked off
from being soaked for so long in the ink and the solvents
he said he often had sharp pains in his stomach

from all of the odors
he said his lungs were filled with methylbenzene
from all of the solvents volatilizing in the air
he said he once took his dripping blood
and used it as red ink to print fifteen pairs of insoles—
in one report of a workplace accident
he said he'd buried in his mind
memories of things that happened in these global factories
when he saw a sports star on TV
leaping high, he'd feel his emotions surge
and his heart quicken, looking
at himself in the mirror
at his aging face and dead eyes
he'd think of that blood when he was twenty
and cry
a few hot turbid tears

East River, Are You Weeping

Walking back and forth
on the banks of the East River
not catching the breeze
not swimming
definitely not looking at the scenery
but going from the print shop and rubber factory
to the hardware factory

Walking back and forth
on the banks of the East River
my baggage comes with me
I go into factory after factory
not quitting jobs
and definitely not on vacation
I'm just
surviving, and survival is hard

spending my time with ink and solvents
spending my time with sulfur, titanium dioxide and colored gum
spending my time with sulfuric acid, rust-removing solvents and powders
spending my time with dirty air and noise

It's like an enormous battlefield
and the sacrifices are: the male and female workers,
and the ink and solvents, sulfur, titanium dioxide, colored gum
sulfuric acid, rust-removing solvents and powders, sweat and blood
all drain down into the sewers
and flow into the vast East River

East River, are you weeping

The Finishing Touch

A component
a component of shoes
a component of sneakers
a component of famous brand sneakers

A printing procedure
a procedure in six steps
to finish
a product component
takes six people
taking turns to finish the coloring
an undertone, white, yellow, black, red, gold
each color and each person takes two to six turns to finish
each turn is another printing
two to six turns to
print, print
print, print, print, print, print, print,
hey, six workers taking turns
print, print,
print, print, print, print, print, print,

hey, six colors taking turns
print, print,
print, print, print, print, print, print,

Hey, we're all hurrying, and in eight hours we finish 2000 pairs
brush, brush brush brush, our sweat flows into the six colors
brush, brush brush brush, our youth dissolves in the six colors
brush, brush brush brush, we imprint soccer wishes into each shoe
brush, brush brush brush, we imprint tennis wishes into each shoe
brush, brush brush brush, we imprint a love of sports into each shoe
brush, brush brush brush, we, China, make shoes that traverse
the seven continents

brush, brush brush brush—
the quality's OK
then the finishing touch:
to dry them
in winds from the seven seas

Train, You Pass Through the Darkness

Father, the year you took me into the coalmine
into a dark world
my young heart didn't dare imagine
that deep in the earth was another complex world
entering through a dark tunnel, working
then exiting through another dark tunnel
I didn't dare imagine that what would come out were real live people
what came out was my father wearing a miner's lamp, his face covered with
soot

I didn't dare imagine, Father
that our family's food and shelter came from a dark tunnel
that place deep in the earth where I walked
Father, the ground under my feet hasn't stopped trembling
many years later, I went south to work in Dongguan
looking for food and shelter in so many factories
each time I take the train from Dongguan to Nanchang
it passes through a dark mountain tunnel
and Father, my heart is still trembling!

Rainy Night

"The dripping sound never stops
and the wind stirs the flesh"

The rain is falling again
it moves my headache
into a humid numb region

Fields of wildflowers in the dark
and no lightning
the lightning doesn't reach the river
but I can see a forest of factories

Each tree is trembling
and someone falls in love with someone from his past:
in one factory
I take my place in the long line for work
and then another
I carry my bags in the train station

What hangs high above
isn't the heart's beacon
it's the workshop where I once shed my blood

If arriving at the truth means shriveling up
I will have no other choice

Watch Factory

I work in a watch factory
the watch factory gives no days off
since time keeps on going and life doesn't stop
our work doesn't stop either

I fit my life into the assembly line
dividing it into lunch and dinner, and breakfast used for a nap
at night working overtime until ten, I adjust the watches' dials to twelve

I have a pure and dream-filled heart, as colorful as the products
we produce Mexican flags, American flags, British flags, pictures of flowers
        and birds,
pictures of rainbows, pictures of castles, pictures of bears eating fish,
        they're all round and pretty
like the faces of many of the female workers. They don't speak
and time keeps on going. Some go to America, some go to Britain, some
        go places I don't know
"It's some foreign country or other,
I heard the boss say everything's exported," Little Fang said.
It's easy to leave a strand of hair inside a watch.
"Those foreigners can tell it's a girl's hair."

No one knows who said that, but Little Fang blushes, and that night she
        talks in her sleep:
"Our lives have to be assembled like watches, with luck and happiness
with love, youth, and the future spinning just like a watch, and it should
        all be wonderful.
But I've heard there's a time difference with foreign countries, here it's
        daytime, over there it's night—"

Severed Finger, No Sound of Crying

Cry as though laughing, and live alongside death.
—Yu Hua, *To Live*

The Girl from Dazhou Who Severed Her Finger
on a Blade Working as a Blade Polisher

The sky is gray, the river flows in torrents
the ordinary workers walk down the ordinary street
the women wear uniforms of every color, walking in twos and threes
to or from rented rooms, factories, hole-in-the-wall stores

Along the Dongshen Channel (people say it leads to Hong Kong) a
hardware factory sits on the manmade banks
on the even number side of the industrial zone, making sunshades to be
exported to America
a few new workers discuss the difference between a beach umbrella and
a coffee shop umbrella
the year was 2006

There was a girl from Dazhou, Sichuan, small with an oval face and
ponytail—
when I went from the workshop to the office I often passed by
the polishing room converted from a stairway
where she worked, lonely, her youth sealed away

She was as simple as a student, sometimes laughing
but more often unable to talk—the noise of the blade polisher
was piercing, earsplitting. After running for awhile it would let off bursts
of sparks
and those little sparks and her small, pretty youth
were enveloped by the dignified factory, sparkling there in the dark

"What are you polishing?" One day I was curious
and drawn in by her girlish smile.

"Blades." She stood there, drawn at any moment into the dark corner
and in the light of the machine console, I saw all different sizes of blades
on the machine
where axe blades are ground beside a basin, and metal-cutting blades are
polished

She said if the depth was adjusted properly it wasn't hard to do, and I saw
her hands
and suddenly realized two of her fingers were missing, and although she
hid them
in that cramped room I felt afraid

Later I heard that her fingers were cut off by blades
as they were polished. Afterward she was posted here, to an easier position

These sharp blades once severed her fingers
and today, she uses the fingers she has left
to polish them anew

A Boy With a Severed Finger Examines His Hand on a Balcony

In Nanya Village along the East River
the opposite shore is covered with streets of bright lights and bars

And a steamer no one in the industrial zone notices
as they mind the products coming down the assembly line

The hardware factory I work in makes watches for countries around the
world
and British flags, American flags,
thermometers for castles, thermometers for barbecues

In 2008, in the extrusion workshop on the first floor
suddenly a girl's scream rose above
the noise of the machines, panic-stricken fish
jumping through the surface of the water

If the bones are crushed, the fingers can't be reattached,
they said, discussing the matter. When he returned from the hospital,
I watched through the window as the boy from Hubei calmly
came in the factory entrance and past the athletic field
everyone's eyes were on him, roasting him like sunlight

Two weeks later, as the sound of card games rose and fell in the next room
I walked in and saw him on the balcony
lifting the hand with the severed finger
using the sky's light
to examine it, and for a long time he didn't lower it

A missing forefinger, like a gun without bullets
like an enormous black hole
that can block out the sunlight

The men playing cards on the iron bunk formed a tight circle
as though he'd been ostracized
"I heard the factory wants to let him go, they're never going to compensate
 him."
"Quit talking about it, his finger fell right next to my foot, I have
 nightmares about it."

For the unmarried boy, this short stop at the hardware factory
brought him a lifetime of pain

No words can do it justice

For My Older Sister Who Lost a Finger Working to Earn My School Fees

Bang bang bang
the sound of impact extrusion
ka ka ka
the sound of the cutter
zi zi zi
the sound of a catch

zi—ka—bang
the sound of a short circuit

In the chaotic workshop
in front of a row of machines
my older sister works her job at a hardware factory at a Pearl Delta port

On January 7, 2015, the day before last,
my sister lost half her forefinger to a machine

"They shaved off the shattered bone, and took a piece of flesh from the
    other hand to replace it."
My sister lies in the hospital, speaking as though about someone else,
there's only one lamp, shining on her injured hand

"I told the boss ages ago that the machine was broken, but he never fixed it."
Then my sister gets angry. What's hard is:
"This year I can't go home for Spring Festival, I'll have to spend it in the
    hospital.
I just returned my train ticket. I was supposed to go home tomorrow."
My sister sighs, thinking of her two children at home
they reunite just once a year, but this time God snatched away her chance

Sister, your hands have picked hot peppers, chopped wood, gathered feed
    for the pigs
Sister, your hands have washed clothes, washed dishes and cooked
Sister, your hands have wiped my childhood butt, wrote letters to me
    when you went off to work, knitted me sweaters
Sister, your hands have worked machines from Yifeng to Dongchang to
    Dongguan to Gaobu to Tangxia to Humen
Sister, your hands have washed dishes in restaurants, made countless brand
    name sneakers and fishing gear and zippers and ornaments in
        factories
Sister, your hands have worked to earn my school fees

Sister, our love is like ten fingers
in pain

Sister, for survival
just to survive, we've given so much
and still our hands are empty

Sister,
now I use my fingers
to wipe away tears

Xin You (1981-2011, Tongshan, Hubei) began writing poetry in 1995. From 1999 to 2004, he worked in Wenling, Zhejiang, then took a job as a business manager in a steel building structure company. In 2010, he took a job at the Women's Federation in Tongshan. On February 20, 2011, he drowned after taking a fall while drunk. *The Collected Works of Xinyou* was published in 2015.

We "Lame Ducks"

We who have no permanent residence
we who make our home wherever we are
we who have left our hometowns
we who float from place to place
we who lead the vagrant life

We who were raised on the yellow earth
who in order to live
betrayed the yellow earth
we who struggle in the city
offering up sweat, dribbling out our youth
often excluded as outsiders

We who scatter to the east and west
we who live in the city
but are still called farmers
we who when we return home
find everything unfamiliar
we who can do two things at once
we who are caught in the middle
we who are abandoned

At the end of the lunar year on the train station platform
we who grip tickets heading back north

and then in the thick springtime of the first lunar month
we who hurry back south one by one

And who exactly are we?
Who exactly are we?

We workers
we who work through the seasons
we who seem like migratory birds who've lost everything

We are those "lame ducks"

Zheng Dong (b. 1981, Tongshan, Hebei) began writing poetry in 2001 when he went to Guangdong to find work. He spent six months working in a hotel, then worked in a plastic dyeing factory, on an assembly line, and in a porcelain factory. In 2014, he moved to Wenzhou to work as a warehouse manager in a shoe factory.

Book of Sorcery

She isn't here, the dim haze
has taken away her breath.
The familiar noises start up,
a cool breeze sweeps against the windows and door,
this isn't summer,
the light in the corners lacks the right heat.
Is it true? It's true, Father says.
The urn can't stroll along the riverside,
it can't look for a boyfriend,
yet another delicate girl loses her life to the crematorium.
A blushing rose broken in the storm,
taken by train straight into the furnace
where there are more fragile women,
and tyrants, icy as steel needles,
tap into their marrow and spirits.
Downtown or at night,
if you listen carefully
you will hear a keen weeping,
and their unceasing incantations:
the sickness tormenting our spirits,
those who officiate and judge wedding certificates,
let plagues and battles flay their rotting bodies,
let our severed fingers make it to California
to collapse in front of the bosses' properties
let them entwine them like ferocious ghosts, generation after generation.

Wu Niaoniao (b. 1981, Huazhou, Guangdong) began writing poetry in 2005. He worked in a film factory in Foshan from 2003 until April 4, 2014, when he was laid off.

Rhapsody on the Advance of Heavy Snow

A snow factory in the sky. Mechanical
assembly line angels, stand day and night in the noise and fluorescent lights
numbly producing beautiful snowflakes
the work overload makes them vomit white froth
while the machines thunder all night. The overload
makes them lose control. The oozing snowflakes
crash down ton after ton. Suddenly my country is a swath of white
and the smiles of thirty provinces are pressed into tears,
the borders are crushed, day and night the army does repairs
and between the earth and sky, only the worker's white heads
are revealed in the blowing snow,
torches and flashlight factories, overtime production
and the temples' destruction. The backs of the gods are also broken
and the faithful followers have long since decamped.
The graves give away the game. The comfortable ghosts
have been forced back into the human world
hugging their gravestones and coffins, admiring the snow
while the threatened earth leans toward that snow-burdened edge
and slowly slowly slowly slowly starts to tilt

Wu Xia (b. 1981, Neijiang, Sichuan) began working in Shenzhen at the age of fourteen. She now works in a clothing factory. Her book of essays is called *Shenzhen Chronicles.*

Sundress

The packing area is flooded with light
the iron I'm holding
collects all the warmth of my hands

I want to press the straps flat
so they won't dig into your shoulders when you wear it
and then press up from the waist
a lovely waist
where someone can lay a fine hand
and on the tree-shaded lane
caress a quiet kind of love
last I'll smooth the dress out
to iron the pleats to equal widths
so you can sit by a lake or on a grassy lawn
and wait for a breeze
like a flower

Soon when I get off work
I'll wash my sweaty uniform
and the sundress will be packed and shipped
to a fashionable store
it will wait just for you
unknown girl
I love you

Bowls Wearing Earrings

The factory cafeteria is lined with
bowls of different patterns. They're sent one by one up to the counter,
and perhaps one will vanish. That's disturbing,
because losing a bowl is like losing one's soul.

Mama bored holes in the sides of her bowl and of mine
and attached loops of iron wire,
so when we pick them up, they shake and clatter.
When I went to get my food, my coworkers laughed and said the bowl
was wearing earrings. But soon they were copying it.
More and more bowls wearing earring appeared in the cafeteria,
like girls just beginning to dress up.
We all worry about losing our jobs,
but the bowls don't have to worry about getting lost.

Who Can Forbid My Love

Outside the train window, lovely scenery rushes past
like a cluster of arrows shot into the heart
the rented room is locked in a dark place

After eighteen years in Shenzhen, my hometown has become unfamiliar
each day I wake up with Shenzhen, and at night we go to sleep together
I love her vigor and vitality, each season brings another round of flowers
evergreen trees and grasses
and I love every inch of her growth. This kind of love seeps
into the pores, skin, cells, blood, bone
even though there's no residence permit with my name on it.

Li Hao (b. 1984, Xixian, Henan) began working construction in 2002. From 2004 to 2007, he studied at Wuhan University. After the Wenchuan earthquake in May of 2008, he participated in the rescue efforts. He now works as an editor for the renowned literary journal *October*. His poetry collections are *Returning Home* and *The Tempest.*

Elegy

—for a fellow worker

Strewn stones and wire mesh at the construction site, the star-filled night
and weeds lead to the road to the county Party seat.
Screw-threads and clasps, calf bones and pigs' feet the stray dogs can't
gnaw through,
fly-bitten chicken intestine and fish viscera rust or rot in the sun,

decomposing each other. Hidden in the dark damp, in the putrefied air, a
watersnake slithers in
from the outlying rice paddies, curling into a ball. The frog in its throat
carefully holds its breath,
facing the long narrow silence that swallowed it alive. In the void, in that
snake's body,

a peripheral column is born, like a distant mountain being moved to a
distant place, like evil forces flying everywhere on the wind,
causing unknown panic and doubt to gush in waves from the rippling rice
fields. My rectified heart
controls my weak will, passing through the forest of scaffolding and
standing on the floorboards, soaked in dim light,

with stayed hands, with steel pipes, it searches for my scattered mind. In
the scaffold we've erected,

with swallows in song, we hurry to put up walls, splitting bricks and time
with bricklayer's cleavers,
irrigating the rifts between life and bricks with cement—blood and sweat,
brick dregs, mortar,

and tempering our penises in our pants.

Suddenly: *kacha!* The singing stops. A burst of vertigo, like a bat streaking
through the air, reversing
its body's perpendicular descent. Then without warning it slams against
the brick wall, between the arrow-straight steel reinforcement bars.
With my own eyes, I see you, singing, hungry. I see you flying through the
air like a scrap of paper.

I see your head and neck and front and back and your cement-covered crotch and your legs straight as arrows piercing the heights and dangling like a harpoon flying into the water and after from the depths emerges a wriggling carp on a crooked bamboo pole

Through the dusk I see your four limbs as though watching a black widow spider on a hemp leaf seizing a locust in its web and all the struggling and I see your hair your face your nostrils mouth and ears and your eyes your chest stomach crotch and your calves and thighs explode outward in a spray: and all of the new songs we sang

pass through your steel bars to your your body to the brick walls we laid together to the cement we spread to roofs of all the buildings to the asbestos tiles to the sand pits to the foundation in the red rust carpet to the earth to the deep stratum until it converges with songs underground and on to the deep purple of blood and the underground dark gushing of an obituary!

You will never more seek in vain for kinsmen. Then, when the call is answered and blocks the gap under the door with lightning and thunder, and from that empty place, alarm bells bring a halt to tears, the rice chaff and farms rising on the other side of the wilderness, you will dwell in our souls. You lie on the thin iron sheeting, stripped of the sun and its aperture, just like your own father.

Ji Zhishui (b. 1984, Taogang, Hubei) graduated from the Hubei Technical School and at nineteen went to work in Guangdong, Zhejiang, and Jiangxi, among other places. She has worked as a dishwasher and weaver, and worked for three years in a battery factory in Guangdong. She now works in a plastics factory in Zhejiang as an assembly line statistician. Her poetry collection is called *Self-Portrait.*

Rocks by the Road

A gust of wind
blows us up from the land
and down onto machines in a strange place, down onto assembly lines
plunged into noise, machine oil, red and black gum, white lead, rust
beaten, screwed tight, nailed up
our quick spinning
flings off our accents and shouts and warm tears
until we can't squeeze out another droplet of sweat
and we harden into rocks
left by the side of the road
even if we go home we don't know how to farm
these rocks piling up by the side of the road
lean against one another, cold against cold

Migrant Workers

These grasses often
encounter a kind of wind
like a basin of cold water being sprinkled out
stripped of a vibrating heartbeat, stripped of a rippling smile
stripped of the most basic respect
we head down
like leaves falling down into the dust
looking for food in the dirt, in garbage piles
these people still want to run, still want to escape
but that only brings them into the trap
others rush onto the knife's point
these grasses are often
thin and weak

Bleeding Fingers

We use them to grasp our bread
to grasp the light that leaks from the cracks in our heads
even to grasp thorny problems
the dripping blood is the life we face
if there's any hope, it's that
the warmth lost along the assembly line
will light up the stars as it scatters
and the screams that burst from the chest
can find an echo in the roaring workshop
let it tremble there
we are washing ourselves spotless
in tears

Ambush

This autumn, the wind blew and the grass wanted to ignite
the clouds brought rain in from a distant city
the mountain stream sweeping past your body and the trees and grasses
sweeps past the crying coming from little earthen houses, the fishing nets,
the primary school
sweeps past the open books, each ink splotch, the poem "Encountering
Sorrow" written with tears and a song…
only dreams get bogged down, wearing the simple garb of spring
piercing through childhood hunger-hallucinations, bringing sleepless
intoxication—
this great northern expanse

You become a weaver, construction worker, electrician, dishwasher…
the days are like a ceremony, forming a kind of connection
the heat of the summer leaves, taking a year's worth of warmth from your
body
your hair catches a bit of the autumn's chilly wind, and they politely inquire
about the unsearchable abyss, this city's waters
where innumerable shadows enter, and come out having exchanged eyes
as though transporting this city's secrets
but the truth resembles other shadows, leaping between tongues, besieging
them
consuming precious words, they're like bullets whizzing past a thirty-year-
old heart
gaining the right to speak. The departed village, the trees and grasses, little
earthen houses, the primary school
each ink splotch on books, tears, they all awaken and arise, to resist the
death all around them: fragile youth

When the night passes, will there be another dawn?
The sound of repeated knocking serves as a long awaited fate
you must open the door, you must
turn on the lamp lying low in your breath

Deaf Workers

I thought the women were the same as me, but if they didn't use their hands
when their words fell, the sound would gather in its wings
I hold my breath, as though listening to a silent rainfall
the words are transparent but weighty, and each time I guess their meanings
the women give me a cheerful thumbs-up
many dark clouds circle over their heads
in the lamp-lit rusty night
their shadows fall on the machines'
concave parts, pinned motionless there
when I walk toward them, their shadows softly fall upon me
as though their weight has been taken by the machines, along with their
        sound
empty, nothing can fill
the single sustaining, imprisoning position
that can provide hope of a freedom without worry
and those words that cannot be voiced are like snowflakes
falling in front of me, flake by flake
ice-cold, but clean and never idle

Old World

After I left my job at the factory
my coat grew old
my shoes faded
I hadn't yet found a new processing plant
or renewed my appearance or repackaged myself
in a new soul
it got older and older, singing of an old world
the sky above me seemed to go back to its old blue
I scrubbed myself until I was clear as glass
there was no longer any need to exchange anything
and there was nothing that could be exchanged
freedom's great victory
in the end meant having nothing

Dinner

In the kitchen, a pair of dirty hands peels potatoes and turnips
stripping off the coarse outer skin. Sometimes only after cutting it open
can you see the rot goes straight to the center

the good parts get chopped and piled up
to be used in flaming stir-fries, doused in heavy oil and salt
or preserved with a few drops of sweat and tears

in front of an exhausted migrant worker
the life that the plate of potatoes or turnips presents
is soft and blurry

in the dusk, a pair of chopsticks
drops under the gradually darkening sky
as though trying to grab the last ray of light

Trial

Pulling open the night of an unfamiliar place
the city's breath roars outside
and the rain is torn by wind, an unstoppable rain, fetid rain
chasing those returning late
with clinking instruments of torture
my gaze follows them, as though
I am running with them
as though the rain is cutting into me
cutting into my soul, cutting into thousands of people
fleeing across the earth and getting washed away
their shadows penetrate a thread of hopelessness and chill
and uncover memory with a practiced touch

On ten acres of riverbank in Wanghu Village
the wind is loudly reading out the verdict
the enormous echo falls on the village's valleys
a few people with withered faces are dragged before the army
no one resists or argues, the people silently recognize the names of the soldiers
I seem to see my sad father
a head that will be held down in the cold wind, lower and lower
the rain and snow will cover them in heavy chains
it is the holes in the fishing nets, the darkness of the caves
that forces the spines to bend
as though one's lifeblood determined this dampness
and one can only bow one's head and admit guilt

More people join this army
in the darkness they chisel away at the ice
the footpaths are obliterated by the laws of wind and snow
my father says less and less, like a leaf dried by the air
the wild wind still roars
it continues to hold its trials
trying him for clutching, for his endlessly wanting hands
and their flowing blood

chiseling fish and springtime out from the ice
under there is a life of enough food and clothing
of spacious warm rooms
of clean dry dreams like clouds
of old age that is not lonely, and medicine to stop the pain

The sharp wind resists the shame of speech
it beats at the ears
beats at that weak man
and the tear-covered skull drops and shatters
burying the dropped notes of teeth and lips in snowdrifts
in the frozen bones
but the wind's deep gasps draw in a group of businessmen
the lamps come on, filling their fat blood-engorged hearts
it beats the trial's gong with fresh blood
but they notice the lake
is no longer a jadeite place bestowed by nature
but a site for a trial
though it looks as silent and calm as before
a group surrounds the men
surrounds the tightened pupils, bitter liquids, the earthen houses and
fishing nets
they curse and hit and kick the fallen skull
they are the executioners
they are the judges
and covetousness is a knife

The last threads of light at night
burn into ashes
the snow covers everything into silence
even those chiseling at the ice are quiet
as though the gloom can dress and calm impatience
and make them seem normal
I hope the highest waves have retreated
and that the spray left behind softly sings a lullaby
sending them back to the riverbank, into warm dreams
may their bitter journeys be over

and all they lack be given to them in their dreams

The corn in the fields is all just husk
they've used up what they had
swaying in the wind, some falling down
like a mother hiding her grief
mother, please let go
of your suffering
has the balmy sun warmed your body
or are you still looking for someone to blame

Go, this lake can't support so many people
go, my youth, my childhood
the wind screams past, the ashes in the fields glint
lighting up pairs of dark eyes
and again the people silently recognize the soldiers' names
and the people return to the dark
longing for the light and sweetness of tomorrow

The wind leads the people toward the running railway tracks
a place of drooping wings
the sun has brought the waterweeds above the surface
there, they melt together with dreams
with heavy colorful lanterns
with the lonely moon
some people enter iron-sheeting workshops, iron-smelting assembly lines
others enter dark pits, coalmines, and even darker apartments
and long strings of numbers obliterate their names

There's nothing to say under fluorescent lights
there's only the overwhelming thundering of the machines
each person nervously faces his or her machine
the whole workshop is still as a narrow ravine
there's only a glimmer of white light, lighting up pairs of flame-leaping wings
and that invisible darkness
drawn into the lungs, the organs, secretly changing the blood

changing the vision and stride
changing marshy dreams
changing the hurting boy, binding up the soul
changing the hands, grasping onto a rice stalk at the edge of the world

In the battery factory, the doubler-plate maker J faints in front of the
machine
and the welder L burns his hand
sweat mixes with red lead power and dust
like tiny earthworms crawling across their faces
crawling into the depths where breath comes from
no matter what, the next day they will return to their machines
returning to their submission, to the fluorescent lights
while others after dinner debate the "unlucky bastards" who have lost hands
and unload the dust from their clothes and leap into the colorful neon
undercurrent

I go to see my father, for a few short minutes
talking about something or other
I just see his white hair
and bloodshot eyes filling with tears
when did father change
into a word that fills me with pain
contact is even worse
the windstorm has stripped him of his last coat of dignity
his bright red hope has fallen away
and his helplessness
fills me with despair

A new year, and the wriggling pupae come out of hibernation
the village butterflies
fly again to their different destinations
the same ones each year, back and forth
the sun is so bright and clear
caressing the red kapok blossoms, the pale green lychee groves
but in the sunless withering workshops and dark apartments
the sky is filled with lead powder, sawdust, cotton fibers

falling into the lungs like breathed-in snow
forcing the tongue silent, and only verdant sweat
runs through the body and howls
here, everyone grows older
and even their movements are stiff in the same way, monotonous
there are only the machines with their blood-thirsty mouths
always ready to swallow
and that missing finger hides exhausted in a corner
no one can hear the noises from outside
middle-aged women workers are frightened into silence
and language is pale and useless anyway
it lies behind a pile of wood
and that old finger in the dark turns deathly pale and curls up
kindling flames and burning the eyes

My father comes back, and the long winter comes to an end
but hesitation and confusion still shine in his eyes
he's still shaken
the way the snow is still falling
the sharp knife of poverty
weakens my old father's bones so he cannot stand straight
like wounded shadows breaking through the soil with spring
thickets of thriving life
with no place to go

Whenever I think of my father, I go to one of the construction sites
all over the city
where I can find workers just like him
wearing rough clothes, their skin dark
and hair white with the snow of life
like leaves hanging
from intricately pattered branches
in the still-tender heights of spring
those in the wind, resisting fruitless labor,
are like gray cattails
stretching out toward the precipice
and when the rainstorms come

those drooping leaves crumble
and tremble

At the X plastics factory, I met a group of truly quiet people
deaf-mute women workers, growing gloomily like little grasses
chewing on the dark, hard night
I always thought they hid themselves, the self
that spoke and acted was somebody else
I liked their happy thumbs-up
and whenever I sensed or guessed their (sign)language,
it seemed I was just like them, happy to find some kind of voice

Plastics worker F, a deaf-mute,
an easily startled, underdeveloped little rabbit
hates any sign of trouble
she pricks up her ears and carefully examines the surroundings with
　　　　bloodshot eyes
sometimes showing two small sharp teeth, keeping her guarded stance
as though something were always heading her way, and she wants to ward
　　　　it off
but she can't ward off overtime without rest, the restless whip
she can't ward off insect holes in the radishes, the enormous insect teeth
she can't ward off the cold frost, the rain and snow
that pulse beneath her heart

An iron nail dyes the floor of the worksite red
the hard kernel of life chooses my father's soles
and he was probably too scared and focused on running
to care where he was going
he tightens his jaw
and his dust-covered hand extracts the iron nail
on the phone he speaks calmly
but what I see is him when he's been drinking
his face red and shadowy
and his eyes drunk
as though the dark night is beautiful
as though tomorrow is nothing to look forward to
he's unsteady on his feet

The factory has people from all over, Guizhou, Henan, Sichuan
but I've never met anyone else from my hometown
I've turned strangers into old friends
in the rushing river current, they're swimming harder than anyone in the city
but with each wave, some go under
some change direction, some suddenly disappear
blown to a faraway place, an even smaller cage
the new machine operator Z is from Yunnan
a meek, careful kangaroo
her background is revealed by her dialect and Mandarin
and just as her tiny feet keep her from running
her smile always comes before her speech
each time she takes a step forward, she says thanks
but she looks like she might fall at any moment
(and she's somehow always losing her tools)
the warehouse managers get fed up with her quiet entreaties
one day, she faints at her machine without warning
they find tumors in her liver and lungs
two days later, she's kicked to the door
only the wind rages, while we stay silent

In one minute, how much wood can be sawed
how many meters of cloth can be woven
how many batteries can be assembled
all this can be calculated
but how much sweat can flow in a minute
how much dust and dark particulate can be taken into the lungs and organs
how many people wander out of their villages
how many fingers are eaten by machines
how many loved ones are separated by blood
that can't be calculated or figured
the calculator and stopwatch stare at me
like I'm an accomplice

Time after time, from one factory to another
you can't escape from the iron circle of fate

like swollen fish
the body is covered with iron gears and scales
worn out from being surrounded by indifference
yearning for the flow of water, a fantasy
covered with cement, gravel, solid steel bars
crucified on patrol by a loaded down body
numb, exhausted
and every time the wind brings clouds overhead
it stirs up longing
but the wind only leaves behind lashings, removing rain and direction
a timid person sinks into an endless dream in the sound of the wind
smoothing the corners, teeth, hammers, daggers of the machines, with
    hometown tides
filling in the empty cement body formed by steel bars
hoping for thunder and lightening
to wash clean and illuminate a deep sleep

My father meets me at the train station
our voices reveal surprise and hesitation
I don't have time to examine his eyes
something else makes my heart ache
he's dyed his white hair black
but can't hide the lines of age on his face
something roils in his eyes, and he turns darker
the hands of time haven't smoothed out those shadows
after I've been away for so long
the cold stays on his body
and on the ground

The bus rattles over the road, my father leans against the window sleeping
he curls up as he dreams
like a child
he's aged, and the years have taken away
his tall shadow, his fine memory
he needs to rest
the rocking bus is like a fishing boat tossed by the waves
or like a child's cradle

in this moment of peace, everything else seems far away
but seeing the white roots of my father's hair
that winter's snow floats in front of me
the snow covers everything and everything is quiet
for growth to come the rain and snow
must be reborn on this suffering earth

Jike Ayou (b. 1985, Puge, Sichuan) is part of the Yi ethnic minority. He attended Chongqing Normal University but left before graduating. He worked for three years in clothing factories in Guangdong, Zhejiang, and Beijing as a down-filler. He began publishing his poetry in 2012, including in his collection *An Yi Worker.* He also started the underground magazine *Yi Workers' Literature.*

Workers in a Typhoon

I come from an Yi Village on Mt. Daliang
and in eastern Zhejiang I encountered a pillager
fanning up wind with its left hand, splashing water with the left,
arrogant and aggressive all the way.
The wild wind harassed the signs,
the heavy letters knocking down pinecones.
Pinecones rolled over the streets,
the frightened cars whistled past,
and the green trees toppled by the roadside behind them,
as the rain came down in sheets to shine their roots.
The river flooded into the heat,
and coworkers spread out fishing nets
in front of their apartments.
The leaves surfed past,
the high-voltage wires cried out in hoots and howls,
the bamboo danced madly.
Workers under their umbrellas were soaked,
running toward the creaking swaying factories.

Late Arrival

For years, I drifted farther than a feather
from Mt. Daliang to Jiaxing, I stuffed feathers into down coats
and when I was called a "dumb duck," I lost the Yi Book of Guidance

For years, the village grew old in my absence
and now it uses the muddy road to Xiaoxingchang
to fight my new shoes and meet my stinging tears

For years, my universe still took the shape of a tiger
as though quoting what Bimo says in the ancient Magor myth
the shivering stockaded village jumped before my eyes and worried me

For years, childhood friends have been building homes
and I've also returned to the center of the earth, and my earthen house
has a three-stone hearth and three main pillars

My father laughs at the fire pit and smokes his long orchid pipe
like a warm book of the classics, I could read it aloud forever,
his walking stick has grown much taller

And my mother laughs in my heart
tonight I want to sleep in her old bed, tonight I must dream
because I came too late to offer sacrifices to the ancestors

Tian Xiaoyin (b. 1985, Baokang, Hubei) graduated from high school in 2004. In 2005, he went to Shanxi to work as a coal miner. From 2007-2009, he worked on an assembly line in a plastics factory in Shanghai, then moved to Shenzhen to be a warehouse manager. In 2011, he moved to Tianjin to take a job in construction. From 2012 on, he returned to Shenzhen and now works in e-commerce and as an editor for a magazine.

I'm Not a Poet, I'm Just a Rebel in May

I bend down slowly
imitating the bent posture of my father tilling the earth
but my grandfather bent down like this and never got back up

That night the village was dark
I stood on a peak and looked down on the castles
then I hung my backpack on the crescent moon's point
I sprinted the length of the village and the distance to the city
counting backwards from my grandfather's grave

In May, I soldered my crumbling bones together
in May I began to rebel
the drawing board's color was mired in mud
hung on one edge was an unfinished line of poetry

I Use Screws to Fix China's Failings

In my imagination my two hands clutch the handle of a hoe
tilling the soil the way our forebears did
intimate with the dust, backs piously bent
then finding the time to go north
to Tiananmen, to see the country
feeling the heart, figuring the distance from the countryside to the palace
saying excitedly: I'm a true Chinese farmer!

And so I ended up abandoned on the road
with thousands upon thousands of sickly people, the color of mud
when the wind changes direction, I slide through the days on wings
flying south

When the swallow's wings are burnt by electric welding
when the oriole's singing is cut short by the assembly line
when the ant's food is poisoned by coal gas
my eyes have already dimmed
the warmer the place the less love is there

Hah!
I'm not a Chinese worker, and I'm not a farmer
my status is that of a man held in suspense
doing an odd job here and there in the south
tightening screws, pounding nails
this is how we fail our poor children
this is the model of Chinese glory
I define myself as: a poet in suspense
I'm trying to pound nails and screws into the failings
I want to ask: China! Is your body hurting?

Makeng Shantytown

Stop at the lowest point of Makeng Shantytown, where everything can be
    hidden
wait for the last leaf to be packed up with thoughts of galloping cold
places luggage has passed, deep traces, we're hoping for a good snowfall

A weakness concealed for twenty years is insulted by your sneeze
gazes and suspicions, doting love and provocations
distorting pain compels me into a solitary rebellious escape

Hallucinogenic ads on bathroom walls, profusions of headlines made by
    massage parlor lamps
scalping and the scalpers are taken in by the era, by the X Bureau....
no lists allowed! Just like Makeng Shantytown is looted by naked animals

Makeng Shantytown is just the bottom of the era's collapse
and I am just an injured ant still screaming in the hole
someday, black and white ants will join in lines and march

I need to go on a long journey. Makeng Shantytown is defined by water
once you leave, you'll never want to go back
in the unknown distance: the yellowing green wheat, green and yellow at
    once

File

Hourly worker. Temporary worker. Contract worker.
Overtime, on duty, consecutive shifts.
That's from my file from Shenzhen. I call it a fictional decipherer.

Zeng Jiqiang (b. 1986, Xinhua, Hunan) began writing poetry in 2002. In 2005 he moved south to Shenzhen and Dongguan, working as a computer technician in an embroidery plant for a year, and then as a spray painter in a toy factory. He has also worked as a warehouse manager and technician. He currently works for a software company in Xiamen.

Here I Gather Up Poetry's Bones

Poetry's flesh has been eaten away
chewed up by pedantic poets
who use sharp teeth to rip it to shreds
these bones of poetry, these cold leftovers
bones that even dogs won't get their noses near
have been tossed into the industrial areas, tossed into the mechanical roar
of the factories
thrown into dim workshops, thrown onto assembly lines
thrown onto the machines, in the midst of helplessness and suffering
no one wants to pick up these stripped bones
"Oh, the great so-and-so...."—the flesh of romantic
poetry! The fresh tender flesh of poetry
smells worse than rotting meat, it isn't for me
it's only good for bloodthirsty ants or for flies.
I peel away the flesh of that poetry
I only want the bones
I want to take wage disputes and backpay, black brick kilns, gas explosions
severed fingers, death, and make it seep into the bare bones. These
abandoned bones are more significant than flesh
none of them know that the calcium in bones
is more nutritious than flesh, more valuable
they don't know that what rots first is the flesh
and what remains is the bones

Xu Lizhi (b. 1990, Jieyang, Guangdong) began working after high school. In 2011, he took a job at the Foxconn plant on the assembly line before being transferred to logistics. He left in 2014 to look for work in Jiangsu, but he was unsuccessful and soon returned to Shenzhen. On September 30 of that year, he jumped to his death. His posthumous collection of poetry is called *A New Day*.

A Laborer Entering the City

Many years ago
with a bag on his back
he walked into
this bustling city

high-spirited and daring

Many years later
he carried his own ashes in his hands
standing at the city's
crossroads

looking around hopelessly

I Speak of Blood

I speak of blood, since it can't be avoided
I also want to speak of breezes, flowers, snow, the moon
speak of the past dynasty, poetry in wine
but reality makes me speak only of blood
blood comes from matchbox rented rooms
narrow, cramped, sunless year round
oppressing the working men and women
distant husbands and wives gone astray
guys from Sichuan hawking spicy soup
old people from Henan selling trinkets on blankets
and me, toiling all day just to live
and opening my eyes at night to write poems
I speak to you of these people, I speak of us
ants struggling one by one through the swamp of life
blood walking drop by drop along the worker's road
blood driven off by the city guards or the choke of a machine
scattering insomnia, illness, unemployment, suicide along the way
the words explode one by one
in the Pearl Delta, in the belly of China
dissected by the seppuku blade of order forms
I speak of this to you
though my voice goes hoarse and my tongue cracks
in order to rip open the silence of this era
I speak of blood, and the sky smashes open
I speak of blood, and my whole mouth turns red

Obituary for a Peanut

Merchandise Name: Peanut Butter
Ingredients: Peanuts, Maltose, Sugar, Vegetable Oil, Salt, Food Additives (Potassium sorbate)
Product Number: QB/T1733.4
Consumption Method: Ready to consume upon opening the package
Storage Method: Before opening keep in a dry place away from sunlight, after opening please refrigerate
Producer: Shantou City Bear-Note Foodstuff Company, LLC
Factory Site: Factory Building B2, Far East Industrial Park, Brooktown North Village, Dragon Lake, Shantou City
Telephone: 0754-86203278   85769568
Fax: 0754-86203060
Consume Within: 18 Months   Place of Production: Shantou, Guangdong Province
Website: stxiongji.com
Production Date: 8.10.2013

Terracotta Army on the Assembly Line

Along the line stands
Xia Qiu
Zhang Zifeng
Xiao Peng
Li Xiaoding
Tang Xiumeng
Lei Lanjiao
Xu Lizhi
Zhu Zhengwu
Pan Xia
Ran Xuemei
these workers who can't tell night from day
wearing
electrostatic clothes
electrostatic hats
electrostatic shoes
electrostatic gloves
electrostatic bracelets
all at the ready
silently awaiting their orders
when the bell rings
they're sent back to the Qin

A Screw Plunges to the Ground

A screw plunges to the ground
working overtime at night
it drops straight down, with a faint sound
that draws no one's attention
just like before
on the same kind of night
a person plunged to the ground

I Swallowed an Iron Moon

I swallowed an iron moon
they called it a screw

I swallowed industrial wastewater and unemployment forms
bent over machines, our youth died young

I swallowed labor, I swallowed poverty
swallowed pedestrian bridges, swallowed this rusted-out life

I can't swallow any more
everything I've swallowed roils up in my throat

I spread across my country
a poem of shame

Afterword

Eleanor Goodman

I first encountered the idea of "worker's poetry" when I heard about the poet Xu Lizhi not long after he committed suicide by jumping out of a building in Shenzhen, where he worked in a Foxconn factory. The suicide drew wide attention, including from the international media, in part because it revealed some of what is behind the many devices so many of us across the world use. These objects are still made partly by human hands including, at one time, Xu Lizhi's.

So when Qin Xiaoyu, the prominent poet, critic, and film director, contacted me and asked me to translate some poems by worker-poets for a film he was co-directing with filmmaker Wu Feiyue, I thought immediately of Xu's story, but also of the workers I encounter wherever I go in China. They sweep the streets, work and sleep on the ubiquitous construction sites, drive the trucks that bring goods into the cities, and clean the floors in restaurants and businesses. These people and certain aspects of the conditions in which they live are obvious: their difficulties are often on display if only one cares to look. What I learned as I began to work on the film *Iron Moon* is just how much is not on display; indeed, most of China's working poor, and in particular, its migrant workers, live large portions of their lives hidden from sight.

These poems, and the documentary film *Iron Moon,* which was inspired by the poetry here, bring readers into migrant workers' homes, workspaces, families, and intimate thoughts, and offer a glimpse of the daily dangers and indignities to which these people are routinely subjected. I say they are hidden because most of us are not allowed to enter their places of work: into deep underground coal mines; into hot, sweaty clothing factories; into factories that produce electronics, paint, shoes, plastic bottles, every consumer good under the sun. These are places that have been deliberately closed off from the public, and for good reason. They are dirty, dangerous, unforgiving places, where illness and injury are common occurrences. But these areas are also closed off because the owners of these mines and factories have every incentive to conceal the conditions their workers deal with day and night.

The poet Chen Nianxi, who worked for over twenty years as a demolitions specialist in mines—a loud, physically demanding, and highly risky job—talks in the film *Iron Moon* about the night he found out his mother had late-stage cancer, knowing that her imminent death will leave his paralyzed father without anyone to care for him. A few lines of his poem "Demolitions Mark" appear on the screen: "My body carries three tons of dynamite / and they are the fuse // Last night / I exploded like the rocks." What could be a more powerful expression of pain, but also of the human will and the determination to carry on?

Shortly after I finished translating the poetry and subtitles in the film, Qin Xiaoyu approached me again with the idea of publishing this anthology of worker's poetry in English. I leapt at the chance. The reason was simple. Having spent eight months with the five poets in the film, I wanted to know more. More about them, more about other worker-poets writing from different vantage points, more about where my clothes and gadgets and Apple products come from. It seems to me a very basic responsibility in this globalized world to try to learn something about the background of all those objects that stock our store shelves and line our closets, to ask questions about the larger chain of production, to be curious about how other people live, and to become more aware of the economic calculations we participate in on a daily basis, largely unconsciously.

These poems offer an opportunity to do just that. May they shock, discomfit, and even anger you. May they bring you into a separate world from your own. And through them, let us all learn more about ourselves and the world we live in.

Qin Xiaoyu

Qin Xiaoyu is a poet, literary critic, and documentary film director. He is the author of the books *Wasting Time, Night Drinking, Long Verse,* and *Jade Ladder: Discussions of Contemporary Chinese Poetry,* among others. He is the editor of *A New Day: The Poetry of Xu Lizhi,* and co-editor with Yang Lian and W.N. Herbert of *Jade Ladder: Contemporary Chinese Poetry* (Bloodaxe Books). He participated in the 2013 Rotterdam Poetry Festival. The film *Iron Moon,* which he wrote and co-directed, was awarded Best Documentary Film at the Shanghai Film Festival and the Guangzhou International Documentary Film Festival.

Eleanor Goodman

Eleanor Goodman is a Research Associate at the Fairbank Center at Harvard University, and spent a year at Peking University on a Fulbright Fellowship. She has been an artist in residence at the American Academy in Rome and was awarded a Henry Luce Translation Fellowship from the Vermont Studio Center. Her first book of translations, *Something Crosses My Mind: Selected Poems of Wang Xiaoni* (Zephyr Press, 2014) was the recipient of a 2013 PEN/Heim Translation Grant and winner of the 2015 Lucien Stryk Prize. The book was also shortlisted for the International Griffin Prize. Her first poetry book, *Nine Dragon Island* (Enclave/Zephyr Press, 2016), was a finalist for the Drunken Boat First Book Prize.

www.ingramcontent.com/pod-product-compliance
Lightning Source LLC
Jackson TN
JSHW021417170426
101040JS00011B/148

* 9 7 8 1 9 4 5 6 8 0 0 3 8 *